Taxcafe.co.uk Tax Guides

Salary versus Dividends

& Other Tax Efficient
Profit Extraction Strategies

Nick Braun PhD

Important Legal Notices:

Published by:
Taxcafe UK Limited
67 Milton Road
Kirkcaldy KY1 1TL
Tel: (0044) 01592 560081
Email: team@taxcafe.co.uk

ISBN 978-1-907302-84-8

14th edition, May 2014

Disclaimer
Before reading or relying on the content of this tax guide please read the disclaimer.

Disclaimer

1. This guide is intended as **general guidance** only and does NOT constitute accountancy, tax, investment or other professional advice.

2. The author and Taxcafe UK Limited make no representations or warranties with respect to the accuracy or completeness of this publication and cannot accept any responsibility or liability for any loss or risk, personal or otherwise, which may arise, directly or indirectly, from reliance on information contained in this publication.

3. Please note that tax legislation, the law and practices of Government and regulatory authorities (e.g. HM Revenue & Customs) are constantly changing. We therefore recommend that for accountancy, tax, investment or other professional advice, you consult a suitably qualified accountant, tax advisor, financial adviser, or other professional adviser.

4. Please also note that your personal circumstances may vary from the general examples provided in this guide and your professional adviser will be able to provide specific advice based on your personal circumstances.

5. This guide covers UK taxation only and any references to 'tax' or 'taxation', unless the contrary is expressly stated, refer to UK taxation only. Please note that references to the 'UK' do not include the Channel Islands or the Isle of Man. Foreign tax implications are beyond the scope of this guide.

6. All persons described in the examples in this guide are entirely fictional. Any similarities to actual persons, living or dead, or to fictional characters created by any other author, are entirely coincidental.

About the Author & Taxcafe

Dr Nick Braun founded Taxcafe in 1999, along with his partner Aileen Smith. As the driving force behind the company, their aim is to provide affordable plain-English tax information for private individuals, business owners and professional advisors.

Over the past 14 years Taxcafe has become one of the best-known tax publishers in the UK and has won several prestigious business awards.

Nick has been a specialist tax writer since 1989, first in South Africa, where he edited the monthly *Tax Breaks* publication, and since 1999 in the UK, where he has authored several tax books including *Property Capital Gains Tax*, *Small Business Tax Saving Tactics* and *Pension Magic*.

Nick also has a PhD in economics from the University of Glasgow, where he was awarded the prestigious William Glen scholarship and later became a Research Fellow.

Contents

Introduction

This guide answers the most common question asked by company owners: "What's the best way to take money out of my company if I want to pay less tax?"

In Part 1 we kick off with a plain English guide to how companies are taxed. We explain how corporation tax is calculated and why companies are such powerful tax shelters.

We then explain how company owners are taxed. As a director/shareholder you can choose the best *mix* of salary and dividends. We examine the pros and cons of each type of income.

Company owners can also choose the most tax efficient *level* of income. We explain how by smoothing your income, or varying it significantly from year to year, you may be able to reduce your tax bill considerably.

In Part 2 we reveal how much tax-free salary and dividend income you can withdraw from your company during the current tax year. You'll discover how couples in business together can pay themselves over £75,000 tax free!

We also explain how you can both protect and maximise your tax-free income from year to year and avoid taking bigger taxable dividends.

If you want to withdraw more income from your company, over and above the tax-free amounts, Part 3 will help you cut your tax bill to the bone.

This part of the guide contains important tax saving strategies for parents who want to avoid the new child benefit tax charge. This kicks in when your income exceeds £50,000 but many company owners will be able to avoid it completely or in part.

There is also important tax planning information for high income earners (those with income over £100,000 or £150,000).

In Part 4 we turn to company owners who have significant amounts of income from other sources (e.g. rental income, other business income and investment income).

We explain why you may need to adjust your company salary or dividends to avoid the higher tax rates that kick in when your income reaches certain key thresholds (£41,865, £50,000, £100,000 and £150,000).

We also examine some tax planning techniques that can be used to reduce or eliminate the tax payable on your other income.

Part 5 looks at the tremendous cashflow benefits of dividends and illustrates how you may be able to postpone paying tax by up to 666 days – enough time to put the money to work and pay off some or all of the tax bill.

In this part of the guide we also explain how you can avoid the dreaded payments on account (early tax payments).

Part 6 explains how company owners can gift shares in the business to their spouses, partners or children and save up to £11,530 in tax this year, with similar savings every year.

We also show how additional tax savings can be achieved by paying tax-free salaries to family members (including minor children) and some of the traps you must avoid when splitting income with other people.

Part 7 looks at some of the best alternative profit extraction strategies including:

- **Directors' loans** – How they can be used to avoid or postpone tax.

- **Rent** – If your company rents a property you own, how much rent should be paid?

- **Pension contributions** – Who should make them, you or the company?

- **Capital gains tax** – How to pay 10% tax when you sell or wind down your company.

In Part 8 we turn to some of the practical issues and dangers that may be experienced when extracting money from your company, including:

- How to avoid the national minimum wage

- How to make sure your salary is a tax deductible expense

- Making sure your company has sufficient distributable profits to declare dividends

- How to declare dividends properly and avoid an HMRC challenge

- The circumstances in which HMRC may try to tax your dividends as earnings

In Part 9 we show how company owners, by altering the amount of income they withdraw from their companies, can reduce the amount of capital gains tax payable when assets like rental properties are sold.

Finally, the last chapter of the guide explains how you may be able to completely avoid tax by emigrating, including details of the new statutory residence test.

Using This Guide & Limitations

This tax guide deals primarily with the 2014/15 tax year which starts on 6 April 2014 and finishes on 5 April 2015.

There are references to other tax years, for example when discussing the advantages and disadvantages of postponing income to a future tax year.

However, it is important to emphasise that the tax rates and tax laws that will apply in future tax years are not known with any degree of certainty.

Tax rates and tax laws (including HMRC's interpretation of those laws) are continually changing. The reader must bear this in mind when reading this guide.

Please note that, although owners of small trading companies are this book's main target audience, this is NOT supposed to be a do-it-yourself (DIY) tax planning guide.

My purpose in writing this guide is to explain in plain English how companies and company owners are taxed and provide some tax planning ideas that can be taken to an accountant or other professional advisor for further discussion.

I do not recommend 'going it alone' when it comes to this type tax planning and there are several reasons for my cautious approach.

Firstly, although the guide covers a fair amount of ground, it does not cover every possible scenario – that would be impossible without making the guide much longer and possibly much more difficult to digest.

In other words, in places I have had to sacrifice definitiveness in favour of making the guide a manageable and hopefully enjoyable read for the average small company owner.

Companies come in many different shapes and sizes, as do their owners, so it is possible that the information contained in this guide will not be relevant to your circumstances.

In particular, please note that this guide is aimed mainly at UK resident director/shareholders who own and work for UK resident companies.

Secondly, the main focus of this tax guide is *income tax* planning: helping company owners pay less tax on their salaries and dividends. There are, however, other taxes that often have to be considered, including capital gains tax and inheritance tax.

Steps that you take to reduce one type of tax can have an adverse impact on your liability to pay other taxes. While some mention is made of other taxes in this guide, I cannot guarantee that all interactions are covered.

Thirdly, there are potential risks involved when it comes to structuring your affairs to reduce the tax payable on salaries, dividends and other payments made by your company.

While most of the tax planning ideas contained in this book are widely used by many accountants and other professional advisers, and have been for many years, this does not mean they have the blessing of HM Revenue & Customs!

There are lots of grey areas when it comes to this area of tax planning and there are no guaranteed tax savings.

In other words, we cannot be certain that some of the tax planning ideas contained in this book will not be subject to some sort of attack from HMRC, even if only at some point in the future.

For example, in the chapters that follow we will show that the most tax-efficient mix of income for most company owners is a small salary coupled with a larger dividend. While this may be the *mathematically* optimal income mix for many company owners, the tax savings are not guaranteed.

There is a danger that HMRC will seek to tax dividends as earnings in some circumstances and may frown on any reduction in an existing salary – see Chapters 30 and 31 for more information.

Fourthly, there are also *non-tax* factors that have to be considered when deciding how much money you withdraw from your company and in what form. In some instances other considerations will outweigh any potential tax savings.

For all of these reasons it is vital that you obtain professional advice before taking any action based on information contained in this guide. The author and Taxcafe UK Ltd cannot accept any responsibility for any loss which may arise as a consequence of any action taken, or any decision to refrain from taking action, as a result of reading this guide

The General Anti-Abuse Rule

A new general anti-abuse rule (GAAR) came into operation on 17 July 2013.

Tax arrangements are "abusive" if they cannot reasonably be regarded as a reasonable course of action – this is commonly referred to as the double reasonableness test.

Clearly it's very subjective and HMRC has sought to reassure taxpayers that there will be a "high threshold" for showing that tax arrangements are abusive:

"There may be a range of views on whether any tax arrangements can be regarded as a reasonable course of action. It is possible that there could be both a reasonably held view that tax arrangements are reasonable and a reasonably held view that the same tax arrangements are unreasonable. In such circumstances the tax arrangements will not be abusive."

An indicator that tax arrangements may not be abusive is if they were "established practice" when entered into and HMRC indicated its acceptance of that practice at the time.

Tax arrangements may be abusive if, for example, the tax result is different to the 'economic' result, for example tax deductions or tax losses that are significantly greater than actual expenses or real economic losses.

If you think that all of the above is a bit vague and subjective, you are not alone. Even the best tax brains in the land don't know what this test means in practice. When legislation contains words like "reasonable" and "abusive" you know you have to be on your guard!

The question being asked by some tax advisers is this: will the anti-abuse rule be used to attack the sort of 'normal' or 'mainstream' tax planning carried out by thousands of small company owners, for example taking small salaries and dividends?

Many tax experts believe that well-established, conventional tax planning will not be attacked by HMRC using the GAAR. Instead the focus will be on the extreme end, for example 'aggressive' or 'artificial' tax avoidance schemes.

However, at present the simple truth is that no one knows how HMRC will apply the anti-abuse rule in practice and whether it will eventually affect many mainstream tax planning practices, including some of those contained in this guide.

Part 1

How Companies & Company Owners Are Taxed

Chapter 1

How Companies Are Taxed

Companies generally pay corporation tax on both their income and capital gains.

There are currently two official corporation tax rates. For the financial year commencing 1 April 2014 the rates are as follows:

- Small profits rate   20%
- Main rate   21%

Companies with taxable profits of £300,000 or less pay 20% corporation tax and companies with taxable profits exceeding £1.5 million pay 21% tax.

If profits are between £300,000 and £1.5 million a 'marginal relief' calculation is made. The practical effect of this is that there are effectively three corporation tax rates:

Profits up to £300,000	20%
Profits from £300,000 to £1.5 million	21.25%
Profits over £1.5 million	21%

For example, a company with profits of £400,000 for the year ending 31 March 2015 will pay 20% on the first £300,000 of profits and 21.25% on the remaining £100,000.

Future Corporation Tax Changes

No changes to the small profits rate have been announced. However, the main rate will fall to 20% in April 2015. The past, current and future corporation tax rates can be summarised as follows:

Profits	Year Commencing 1 April		
	2013	2014	2015
Up to £300,000	20%	20%	20%
£300,000 to £1.5 million	23.75%	21.25%	20%
Over £1.5 million	23%	21%	20%

11

Associated Companies

The corporation tax profit bands must be divided up if there are any 'associated companies'. The basic rule is that a company is associated with another company if they are both under the control of the same person.

For example, if you own all of the shares in two companies these companies will be associated. Each company will start paying corporation tax at 21.25% when its profits exceed £150,000 (i.e. £300,000/2). If there are three associated companies, this higher rate will kick in at £100,000 (£300,000/3)... and so on.

Companies controlled by close relatives or business partners are also counted as associated companies if there is a substantial commercial relationship between the companies.

The associated company rules will become much less important in April 2015 when the main rate of corporation tax is reduced to 20% and unified with the small profits rate. Business owners will no longer have an incentive to spread their activities across several companies to avoid paying corporation tax at the main rate. A few years ago, when the main rate was 30% and the small profits rate was 19%, there was an incentive to own lots of small companies rather than one large one.

The associated company rules will still be relevant for other purposes, for example in deciding whether a company has to pay corporation tax in quarterly instalments. Instalments are generally payable by companies whose profits exceed £1.5 million but this amount is divided up if there are any associated companies.

Whereas small companies only have to pay their corporation tax nine months after the financial year has ended, companies subject to instalments have to start paying tax half way through the year.

The associated company rules will be replaced with a simpler "51% group test" in April 2015. If a company owns at least 51% of, say, three subsidiaries, the four companies will be "associated" and the £1.5 million profit limit will be divided by four to determine whether corporation tax has to be paid in instalments.

Throughout this guide, the focus is mainly on the tax position of a single company with no active associated companies.

Trading Companies vs Investment Companies

In tax jargon a 'trading' company is one involved in, for want of a better word, 'regular' business activities, e.g. a company that sells goods online, a catering company or a firm of garden landscapers. Common types of *non-trading* company include those that hold substantial investments in property or financial securities or earn substantial royalty income.

Corporation Tax

If your company is involved 'wholly or mainly' in non-trading activities it could be classed as a close investment holding company (CIC). CICs pay corporation tax at the main rate, currently 21%, on ALL of their profits, including their existing trading profits. They cannot benefit from the 20% small profits rate. Of course, with a mere 1% difference between the main rate and small profits rate, this is no longer much of a penalty and will be irrelevant from April 2015 when the two corporation tax rates are merged.

Companies that invest in rental property are specifically excluded from the CIC provisions. This means they can enjoy the 20% corporation tax rate (unless there is private use of the properties by the owner and his family or they are let to connected persons).

Capital Gains Tax

If a company has too many non-trading activities (including most property investment and property letting) it may lose its trading status for capital gains tax purposes.

This will result in the loss of two important CGT reliefs:

- Entrepreneurs Relief
- Holdover Relief

Entrepreneurs Relief allows you to pay capital gains tax at just 10% when you sell your company, as opposed to 28% (see Chapter 25).

Holdover Relief allows you to give shares in the business to children, common-law spouses and other individuals free from CGT. (You don't need Holdover Relief to transfer shares to your spouse because such transfers are always exempt.)

Although owning rental properties will not affect the company's corporation tax rate, it can affect the company's CGT rate.

The company will, however, only lose its trading status for CGT purposes if it has 'substantial' investment activities. Unfortunately to the taxman 'substantial' means as little as 20% of various measures such as:

- Assets
- Turnover
- Expenses
- Profits
- Directors' and employees' time

HMRC may attempt to apply the 20% rule to *any* of the above measures.

Inheritance Tax

Shares in trading companies generally qualify for business property relief which means they can be passed on free from inheritance tax. However, if the company holds investments (including rental property) this could result in the loss of business property relief.

The qualification criteria are, however, more generous than for CGT purposes and a company generally only loses its trading status for inheritance tax purposes if it is 'wholly or mainly' involved in investment related activities.

To be on the safe side you may want to ensure that the company's qualifying activities exceed 50% of each of the measures listed above (e.g. turnover, time, profits etc).

For more information see our guide *How to Save Inheritance Tax*.

Accounting Periods vs Financial Years

A company's own tax year (also known as its 'accounting period') may end on any date, for example 31 December, 31 March etc.

Corporation tax, on the other hand, is calculated according to financial years. Financial years run from 1 April to 31 March.

The 2014 financial year is the year starting on 1 April 2014 and ending on 31 March 2015.

Why is this important? For starters, it's often useful to be aware of the official terminology, for example when talking to your accountant or when reading HMRC's official documentation. It may also be important when calculating how much tax your company will pay, especially when corporation tax rates change from one financial year to the next.

For example, on 1 April 2014 the main rate of corporation tax fell from 23% to 21%. A company with over £1.5 million of taxable profits, whose accounting period runs from January 2014 to December 2014, will therefore pay corporation tax as follows:

- 3 months to 31 March 2014   23%
- 9 months to 31 December 2014   21%

The practical effect is that the company will pay 23% corporation tax on approximately one quarter of its profits and 21% tax on three quarters of its profits. (It doesn't matter at what point during the financial year the profits are actually made.) This means the company's *effective* corporation tax rate is 21.5%.

Companies with profits of £300,000 or less pay corporation tax at the small profits rate. The rate is currently 20% and no changes have been announced for future years. So for these companies it is not necessary to do two corporation tax calculations. Corporation tax will be payable at a flat rate of 20% on all of the company's profits, even if the accounting period straddles two financial years.

Companies as Tax Shelters

This guide shows company owners how to extract money from their companies in the most tax efficient manner possible. However, before progressing to the various profit extraction strategies it is worth reiterating why it may be advantageous to use a company in the first place.

The corporation tax paid by a company is often far lower than the income tax and national insurance paid by self-employed business owners (sole traders and partnerships).

Self-employed business owners face the following combined income tax and national insurance rates (2014/15 figures):

First £5,885	£0
£5,885 to £7,956	£143
£7,956 to £10,000	9%
£10,000 to £41,865	29%
£41,865 to £100,000	42%
£100,000 to £120,000	62%
£120,000 to £150,000	42%
Over £150,000	47%

How do these tax rates compare with the corporation tax payable by companies?

Table 1 compares the total tax paid by self-employed business owners and companies at different profit levels:

TABLE 1
Self-Employed vs Corporation Tax 2014/15

Profits	Self Employed	Company	Saving
£10,000	£327	£2,000	-£1,673
£20,000	£3,227	£4,000	-£773
£30,000	£6,127	£6,000	£127
£40,000	£9,027	£8,000	£1,027
£50,000	£12,985	£10,000	£2,985
£60,000	£17,185	£12,000	£5,185
£70,000	£21,385	£14,000	£7,385
£80,000	£25,585	£16,000	£9,585
£90,000	£29,785	£18,000	£11,785
£100,000	£33,985	£20,000	£13,985

Clearly a company itself does not always pay less tax than a self-employed business owner, especially when profits are small. However, as profits increase so do the tax savings.

For example, when the profits of the business reach £100,000 a tax saving of £13,985 is achieved by the company.

A business owner who uses a company will therefore have potentially far more after-tax profit left to reinvest and grow the business. It is in these circumstances – when profits are reinvested – that companies are normally most powerful as tax shelters.

Profit Extraction = Additional Tax?

Table 1 may be misleading because it compares the total tax payable by a self-employed business owner with the corporation tax payable by a company. We haven't started looking at the tax treatment of income extracted by the company owner.

Most company owners need to extract money for their own personal use. At this point an additional income tax and national insurance charge *may* arise.

The good news is that by carefully structuring your pay it is possible to minimise and in some cases avoid these additional tax charges. That's what this guide is all about!

If you own a company that is currently making modest profits (under £30,000 say), you may be looking at Table 1 and thinking: "I could save more tax if I was self employed!"

As we shall see shortly, however, it is possible for a director/shareholder to receive a small salary that is completely tax free *and* reduces the company's corporation tax bill because it is a tax deductible expense.

Most small companies will see their corporation tax bills fall by around £1,600 by paying these tax-free salaries, making a company potentially attractive at lower profits levels.

Chapter 2

How Directors Are Taxed: Employment Income

When HMRC and tax professionals talk about 'employment income', they are referring to salaries and bonuses.

Salaries and bonuses are subject to income tax and national insurance. They are also generally a tax deductible expense for the company.

Income Tax

For the 2014/15 tax year, starting on 6 April 2014, most individuals pay income tax as follows on their salaries:

- 0%   first   £10,000   Personal allowance
- 20%   next   £31,865   Basic-rate band
- 40%   above   £41,865   Higher-rate threshold

Generally speaking, if you earn more than £41,865 you are a higher-rate taxpayer; if you earn less you are a basic-rate taxpayer.

The number £41,865 is important to remember because it will be mentioned repeatedly in the chapters that follow.

Income over £100,000

When your taxable income exceeds £100,000 your income tax personal allowance is gradually withdrawn. For every additional £1 you earn, 50p of your personal allowance is taken away.

What this means is that, when your income reaches £120,000, your personal allowance will have completely disappeared.

It also means that those who earn salary income between £100,000 and £120,000 face a marginal income tax rate of 60%.

Example

Caroline, a company director, has received salary income of £100,000 so far during the current tax year.

If she receives an extra £100 of salary she will pay an extra £40 of income tax. She will also lose £50 of her income tax personal allowance, so £50 of previously tax-free salary will now be taxed at 40%, adding £20 to her tax bill.

All in all, she pays £60 in tax on her extra £100 of salary, so her marginal income tax rate is 60%.

Income above £150,000

Once your taxable income exceeds £150,000, you will pay 45% income tax on any extra employment income. This is known as the additional rate of tax. It used to be 50%.

National Insurance

For the current 2014/15 tax year most individuals pay national insurance as follows on salary income:

- 0%   on the first   £7,956   Primary threshold
- 12% on the next   £33,909
- 2%   above   £41,865   Upper earnings limit

Combined Tax Rates

The combined marginal rates of income tax and national insurance applying to salaries in 2014/15 are as follows:

Income up to £7,956	0%
Income from £7,956 to £10,000	12%
Income from £10,000 to £41,865	32%
Income from £41,865 to £100,000	42%
Income from £100,000 to £120,000	62%
Income from £120,000 to £150,000	42%
Income over £150,000	47%

Employer's National Insurance

Most employees don't lose sleep over their employer's national insurance bill. However, as a company director/shareholder, the company's money is effectively your money so this extra tax is an important consideration.

Companies pay 13.8% national insurance on every single pound of salary the director/shareholder earns over £7,956.

Employer's national insurance is, however, a tax deductible expense for corporation tax purposes. For example, if a small company pays £100 of national insurance this will reduce its taxable profits by £100, saving the company £20 in corporation tax (£100 x 20% = £20). So the net overall cost is £80.

£2,000 Employment Allowance

Most businesses qualify for the new employment allowance, which provides a saving of up to £2,000 per year in employer's national insurance.

Most business tax cuts in recent times (for example, cuts in corporation tax rates and increases in the annual investment allowance) have only helped *big businesses*. The employment allowance provides a cash boost to all businesses that employ people.

The reason for covering the employment allowance in this guide is because it may affect some company owners' choice of salary. For example, a company owner who has no other employees can pay himself a salary of up to £22,449 this year without having to pay any employer's national insurance.

But is it a good idea to take this much salary to avoid wasting the £2,000 employment allowance? We'll answer this question in Chapter 6. In this section we'll take a brief look at some of employment allowance rules.

The employment allowance can only be used against class 1 national insurance and not against class 1A national insurance. Class 1A is due on most taxable benefits provided to employees, e.g. company cars.

If your company belongs to a group of companies, only one can claim the allowance. If your business runs multiple PAYE schemes, the allowance can only be claimed against one scheme.

The allowance is claimed as part of the payroll process. The full £2,000 can be claimed in month one of the tax year if your employer's class 1 national insurance exceeds £2,000 per month.

You can start claiming the allowance after the tax year has started and make a catch-up claim which can also be offset against your other PAYE costs. For example, let's say your company has PAYE costs of £1,300 per month made up of £500 employer's national insurance and £800 of other PAYE costs such as employees national insurance.

Let's also say you start claiming the employment allowance a few months into the tax year, when your claim to date would have been £1,500 (£500 x 3). This is enough to cover your employer's national insurance and other PAYE liabilities for the current month, leaving a balance of £700 (£2,000 - £1,300) that can be offset against next month's employer's national insurance and other PAYE liabilities.

If you claim the allowance at the end of the tax year and your remaining PAYE costs are not sufficient to use the entire allowance, the unclaimed balance can be carried forward to the next tax year.

Connected Companies

A company cannot claim the employment allowance if a 'connected company' already claims it. Companies are connected if one company has control of the other company or both companies are controlled by the same person.

A person is generally considered to have control of a company if they hold more than 50% of the company's share capital or voting power or if they are entitled to more than 50% of the company's distributable income or assets if the company is wound up. For example, if you own all the shares in two companies you will only be entitled to one employment allowance, even if the two companies are completely separate businesses with, for example, separate premises and staff.

22

If the company that claims the employment allowance has employer's class 1 national insurance of less than £2,000, the balance cannot be claimed by the other company.

Where there is 'substantial commercial interdependence' between two or more companies the holdings of close relatives and other 'associates' are added together to determine whether they are controlled by the same person or group of persons.

For example, if you own all the shares in company X and your spouse owns all the shares in company Y, your spouse's holding in company Y is attributed to you and you are treated as controlling company X and Y, as is your spouse. However, the two companies will only be treated as connected companies if there is substantial commercial interdependence between them.

If the two companies are completely unrelated then two employment allowances can be claimed. If there is substantial commercial interdependence between the companies then only one allowance can be claimed.

The definition of associates is broad but would typically include spouses, parents and grandparents, children and grandchildren, brothers and sisters, business partners and certain trusts.

To determine whether there is substantial commercial interdependence between two companies one or more of the following must be present:

- **Financial interdependence** – Two companies are financially interdependent if one gives financial support to the other or each has a financial interest in the same business.

- **Economic interdependence** – Two companies are economically interdependent if they have the same economic objective or the activities of one benefits the other or they have common customers.

- **Organisational interdependence** – Two companies are organisationally interdependent if they have common management, employees, premises or equipment.

Case Study – Total Tax Payable on Salary

Jane owns a company and takes a salary of £60,000. Her income tax for 2014/15 can be calculated as follows:

- 0%   on the first   £10,000   =   £0
- 20% on the next   £31,865   =   £6,373
- 40% on the final   £18,135   =   £7,254

Total income tax bill: £13,627

Her national insurance for 2014/15 can be calculated as follows:

- 0%   on the first   £7,956   =   £0
- 12% on the next   £33,909   =   £4,069
- 2%   on the final   £18,135   =   £363

Jane's national insurance bill: £4,432.

Her company claims the £2,000 employment allowance but this is used up paying salaries to other employees. Her company's national insurance bill on her salary is therefore:

- 0%   on the first £7,956   =   £0
- 13.8% on the next £52,044   =   £7,182

The company's national insurance bill is £7,182. If we assume that Jane's company pays corporation tax at 20%, the company's national insurance bill, net of corporation tax relief, is £5,746.

The total tax paid by Jane and her company is as follows:

	£
Income tax	£13,627
Employee's national insurance	£4,432
Employer's national insurance	£7,182
Total taxes	£25,241

When you include employer's national insurance, it's startling how much tax is paid on Jane's income. Her £60,000 salary is not low by any standards but you wouldn't describe her as a high income earner either. Nevertheless an amount equivalent to 42% of her salary is paid in direct taxes on her income.

Future Income Tax Changes

In the March 2014 Budget, it was announced that income tax will be levied as follows in the 2015/16 tax year:

- 0% on the first £10,500 Personal allowance
- 20% on the next £31,785 Basic-rate band
- 40% above £42,285 Higher-rate threshold

The personal allowance will continue to be withdrawn when your income exceeds £100,000 and will be completely taken away if your income exceeds £121,000.

No changes have been announced to the 45% additional rate that applies to income over £150,000.

Transferable Personal Allowance for Married Couples

Starting in 2015/16 it will be possible to transfer up to £1,050 of unused personal allowance to your spouse or civil partner. Unmarried couples will not be able to use this tax break.

To be eligible neither person must be a higher-rate or additional-rate taxpayer. In other words, to benefit one spouse must earn less than £10,500 and the other must earn less than £42,285.

From 2016/17 onwards, the transferable amount will be 10 per cent of the personal allowance.

Example
In 2015/16 Bill earns a salary of £30,000 and his wife Daphne earns £6,000 working part time. Daphne has £4,500 of unused personal allowance. She can transfer £1,050 of this to Bill which means Bill no longer has to pay tax on £1,050 of his income. This will save him £210 in tax (£1,050 x 20%).

Claims are to be made online and couples will receive the benefit from the summer of 2016.

Chapter 3

How Directors Are Taxed: Dividend Income

Dividends are subject to income tax but not national insurance.

Income tax rates on dividends are lower than income tax rates on salaries because dividends are paid out of a company's *after-tax* profits: the money has already been taxed in the company's hands, whereas salaries are a tax deductible expense.

The income tax rates applying to *cash dividends* in 2014/15 are:

- Basic-rate taxpayers   0%
- Higher-rate taxpayers   25%
- Additional rate taxpayers   30.6%

By cash dividends we mean the actual payment from the company to the director/shareholder.

Gross Dividends vs Cash Dividends

As we know from Chapter 2 you become a higher-rate taxpayer when your income exceeds £41,865. And if your income exceeds £150,000 you become an additional-rate taxpayer.

However, those thresholds are for *gross* dividends, not the actual *cash* dividends you receive from your company.

Whereas company owners are mostly interested in their cash dividends (the money they actually withdraw from their companies), most tax calculations work with gross dividends.

If you want to minimise the income tax payable on your dividend income it is essential to understand the difference between gross dividends and cash dividends.

Gross dividends are found by dividing cash dividends by 0.9:

Gross dividends = Cash dividends/0.9

Similarly, cash dividends are found by multiplying gross dividends by 0.9:

Cash dividend = Gross dividend x 0.9

For example, if you pay yourself a cash dividend of £90, the gross dividend is £100 (£90/0.9).

The £10 difference is what's known as the dividend tax credit.

Gross dividends are taxed at the following rates:

- Basic-rate taxpayers   10%
- Higher-rate taxpayers   32.5%
- Additional rate taxpayers   37.5%

However, to calculate the final income tax bill you subtract the 10% dividend tax credit. The dividend tax credit is supposed to compensate company owners for the fact that dividends are paid out of profits that have already been subjected to corporation tax.

The *effective* income tax rates on gross dividends are as follows:

- Basic-rate taxpayers   0%
- Higher-rate taxpayers   22.5%
- Additional rate taxpayers   27.5%

It's all unnecessarily complicated – a bit like climbing over a mountain instead of walking around the side – but UK tax law carries a lot of baggage like this from years gone by.

However, you do have to understand how dividends are taxed if you want to minimise the income tax payable on them!

Example

Robert is a company owner with a salary of £10,000 in 2014/15. The company pays him a cash dividend of £50,000. His income tax is calculated as follows:

	£
Salary	*10,000*
Cash dividend	*50,000*
Tax credit (£50,000 x 1/9)	*5,555.56*
Gross dividend	*55,555.56*
Less: personal allowance	*(10,000)*
Taxable income	*55,555.56*
Basic-rate band: £41,865 - £10,000	*31,865*
Income tax @ 10%	*3,186.50*
Subject to higher rate tax:	
£55,555.56 - £31,865	*23,690.56*
Income tax @ 32.5%	*7,699.43*
Total income tax	*10,885.93*
Less: tax credit	*(5,555.56)*
Income tax due	*5,330.37*

Robert's income tax can be calculated much more quickly by remembering that higher-rate taxpayers effectively pay 22.5% tax on gross dividends over the £41,865 higher-rate threshold. For example, we know Robert's total income is £65,556:

£10,000 salary + £55,556 gross dividends = £65,556

The amount of income subject to higher rate tax is £23,691:

£65,556 - £41,865 = £23,691

The total income tax is therefore £5,330:

£23,691 x 22.5% = £5,330

(The above numbers have been rounded for simplicity.)

If your other non-dividend income is less than £10,000 (2014/15), part of your dividend income will be covered by your income tax personal allowance.

However, this will not produce an additional tax saving because the dividend tax credit is also restricted (essentially you cannot double up the tax-free amount). The dividend tax credit is restricted to 10% of taxable income.

Example revised

Robert is a company owner with a salary of £7,956 in 2014/15. The company pays him a cash dividend of £50,000. His income tax bill is calculated as follows (numbers rounded for simplicity):

	£
Salary	*7,956*
Cash dividend	*50,000*
Tax credit (£1,000 x 1/9)	*5,556*
Gross dividend	*55,556*
Personal allowance	*(10,000)*
Taxable	*53,512*
Remaining basic-rate band:	
£41,865 - £10,000	*31,865*
Income tax @ 10%	*3,187*
Subject to higher rate tax:	
£53,512 - £31,865	*21,647*
Income tax @ 32.5%	*7,035*
Total income tax	*10,222*
Less: tax credit (restricted)	*5,351*
Income tax due	*4,871*

Again Robert's income tax can be calculated much more quickly by remembering that higher-rate taxpayers effectively pay 22.5% income tax on their gross dividends.

For example, we know his total income is £63,512:

£7,956 salary + £55,556 gross dividends = £63,512

The amount of income subject to higher rate tax is therefore £21,647:

£63,512 - £41,865 = £21,647

The total income tax is therefore £4,871:

£21,647 x 22.5% = £4,871

Confusing Gross Dividends and Cash Dividends

If you want to ensure that your dividend income does not breach the £41,865, £100,000 or £150,000 thresholds it is critical to remember that it is the *gross dividend* that is relevant, not the cash dividend actually received.

Example

Matthew is a company owner with no other taxable income for the year. He decides to pay himself a cash dividend of £40,000, under the mistaken belief that he will pay 0% tax because his income is below the higher-rate threshold (£41,865 in 2014/15).

However, Matthew's gross dividend income is actually £44,444 and his income tax bill is £580:

£40,000/0.9 = £44,444 - £41,865 = £2,579 x 22.5% = £580

Chapter 4

Salary versus Dividends: The Basics

Unlike self-employed business owners (sole traders and partnerships), company owners are in the fortunate position of wearing two caps.

On the one hand, you can reward your work as a director; on the other hand, you can reward your entrepreneurship as a shareholder.

As a company director and shareholder you can split your income into salary and dividends and this could generate large income tax and national insurance savings.

For example, while national insurance is payable on salaries, it is not payable on shareholder dividends.

By structuring distributions from your company carefully and taking the 'optimum' amount of salary and dividends, you could end up with a significantly higher after-tax income than a regular salaried employee who earns a higher income before-tax.

However, while saving income tax will be an important consideration, other factors are important too.

Salaries & Dividends: What's the Difference?

The major differences between a salary and dividend are the following:

Salaries Are Tax Deductible

Salaries usually qualify for corporation tax relief, dividends do not.

If the company pays you a salary, its taxable profits will be reduced and it will pay less corporation tax.

Dividends are paid out of a company's after-tax profits, so paying a dividend does not reduce the *company's* tax bill.

This is an important point to remember because most company owners are concerned about both their own and their company's tax bill.

For example, if a company has a taxable profit of £10,000 it will pay £2,000 in corporation tax (20%), leaving £8,000 available to distribute as dividends.

Even if the company's shareholders pay no income tax on their dividends, they have effectively suffered 20% tax on their income.

Dividends Require Profits

Only companies that have made profits can pay dividends. Profits are usually calculated when the company's annual accounts are drawn up (often many months after the end of the company's financial year).

So dividends will usually be paid out of profits made in a previous accounting period. It is, however, possible to pay dividends out of profits made during the current year, for example if accurate management accounts are drawn up to determine the level of the company's distributable profits (see Chapter 29).

Salaries can be paid even if the company is making tax losses.

National Insurance

Salaries are generally subject to national insurance, dividends are not. Both the director and the company may be subject to national insurance.

Income Tax

Salaries and dividends are subject to different rates of income tax.

Tax Payment Dates

The income tax and national insurance payable on salaries is collected almost immediately via PAYE. The income tax on dividends is collected via self assessment – generally at a much later date.

Earnings

Salaries are classed as 'earnings' which is important if you want to make significant pension contributions. Dividends are not classed as earnings (see Chapter 24).

Chapter 5

Company Owners Can Control Their Income Tax Bills

In Chapter 4 we mentioned that a company owner can often decide whether any distribution of the company's money is classified as salary or dividend.

Another advantage of being a company owner is that you have complete control over *how much* income you withdraw in total.

This gives you significant control over your personal income tax bill.

Unlike sole traders, who pay tax each year on ALL the profits of the business, company owners only pay income tax on the money they actually withdraw from the company.

This allows company owners to reduce their income tax bills by adopting the following strategies:

- 'Smooth income'
- 'Roller-coaster income'

Smooth Income

With smooth income, the company owner withdraws roughly the same amount of money each year, even though the company's profits may fluctuate considerably.

'Smooth income' allows the director/shareholder to stay below any of the following key income tax thresholds that could result in a higher income tax bill:

- £41,865   Higher-rate tax
- £50,000   Child benefit tax charge
- £100,000   Personal allowance withdrawal
- £150,000   Additional rate tax

We will return to how you can plan your salary and dividend withdrawals around these key income tax thresholds in the chapters that follow.

The last three thresholds didn't even exist a few years ago, which goes to show how much more complicated and burdensome the UK's income tax system has become for those considered to be 'high earners'.

Roller-coaster Income

With 'roller-coaster income', the directors/shareholders take a bigger or smaller salary or dividend than would normally be required to fund their lifestyles.

Roller-coaster income could save you tax in the following circumstances:

Tax Rates Are Going Up Or Down

If the Government announces that tax rates will *rise* during a future tax year, you may wish to pay yourself more income now and less income later on.

And if your tax rate will *fall* during a future tax year, you should pay yourself less income now and more income later on.

Two recent tax changes that we were all warned about well in advance include the child benefit charge and the reduction in the additional rate of tax from 50% to 45%.

You Want to Avoid Capital Gains Tax

It may also make sense for company owners to pay themselves less income during tax years in which they sell assets subject to capital gains tax, e.g. rental properties.

Why? This may allow some of your basic-rate band (£31,865 in 2014/15) to be freed up, which means some of your capital gains will be taxed at 18% instead of 28% (see Chapter 33).

Living Abroad

If you intend to move abroad and become non-resident in the future, you could consider withdrawing less income from your company while you are UK resident and more income after you become non-resident.

Providing you move to a country with favourable income tax rates, this strategy could potentially save you significant amounts of UK income tax (but see Chapter 34 for potential dangers).

Pension Income

When you reach age 55 you may decide to start withdrawing money from any private pension scheme you belong to, for example a self-invested personal pension (SIPP). Any amount you withdraw over and above your 25% tax-free lump sum will be subject to income tax.

Fortunately, if you opt for a pension drawdown arrangement, you can vary the amount of income you withdraw from your pension scheme every year (from April 2015 there will be no limits placed on the amount of income you can withdraw).

Coupled with the fact that you can vary the amount of income you withdraw from your company, this could allow you to minimise your income tax bill by staying below any of the income tax thresholds listed earlier.

Part 2

Tax-free Salaries & Dividends

Chapter 6

Tax-free Salaries

After reading the preceding chapters you should have a good understanding of how salaries and dividends are taxed.

The next question is: What is the most tax-efficient mix of salary and dividends for directors/shareholders who want to extract money from their companies?

In the next few chapters we will illustrate how much *tax-free* salary and dividend income company owners can withdraw from their companies.

In this chapter we begin with the optimal amount of tax-free salary.

All amounts are for the current tax year which ends on 5 April 2015. The answer changes every year, so make sure you stay up to date.

Assumption: No Other Taxable Income

We will assume for now that the director/shareholder has no other taxable income. This keeps the number crunching as simple as possible.

It's not a totally unrealistic assumption either. Although most company directors have at least some other taxable income, for example some bank account interest or stock market dividends, many have no more than a few hundred pounds.

For those director/shareholders who do have significant amounts of other taxable income, for example rental profits from a portfolio of properties, more information is provided in Part 4.

Why a Small Salary Is Tax Efficient

The first point to make is that most company owners should not pay themselves just dividends and no salary.

The first few thousand pounds of either salary or dividends are tax-free in the hands of the director/shareholder, if the payments fall within the various income tax and national insurance thresholds.

However, a dividend payment is not necessarily tax efficient for the *company* (and, of course, most company owners are equally concerned about their company's tax position as their own personal tax position).

Dividends are paid out of a company's *after-tax* profits, i.e., after corporation tax has been paid. So every dividend has a corporation tax bill attached to it.

A salary, on the other hand, is a tax deductible expense for the company. Salaries are subject to employer's national insurance but this only kicks in when the salary exceeds £7,956. Salaries below this threshold have no national insurance consequences.

In summary, a small salary is much more tax efficient than a dividend. Not only is it tax free in the hands of the director/shareholder, it provides a corporation tax saving for the company as well.

This corporation tax saving is essentially a cashback for the company and is why the director/shareholder should consider paying a salary, even if the money isn't needed.

For the same reason, the director/shareholder should consider paying salaries to their spouse or partner and children, including their minor children, wherever possible (see Part 6).

How Much Salary?
Companies with Employees
(i.e. with no spare employment allowance)

We will start off here with company owners whose £2,000 employment allowance (see Chapter 2) is already used up paying salaries to other employees, i.e. there is no spare employment allowance for the directors own salaries.

We will also assume that the company has profits of £300,000 or less and therefore pays 20% corporation tax.

Companies with higher profits face a higher corporation tax rate and we will take a closer look at them shortly.

So how much salary should a company owner in this situation take? There are two important income tax and national insurance thresholds for the current 2014/15 tax year:

- National insurance   £7,956
- Income tax   £10,000

For the 2014/15 tax year the most tax efficient salary for directors of companies with no spare employment allowance is £7,956.

A salary of £7,956 will not attract any employee's or employer's national insurance and, providing the director/shareholder has no other income, it will also be free from income tax.

Because salary payments are usually a tax deductible business expense, a salary of £7,956 will also save the company £1,591 in corporation tax:

£7,956 x 20% corporation tax = £1,591

In other words, it will cost the company just £6,365 to put £7,956 of tax-free cash in the hands of the director/shareholder.

Salary of £10,000?

Why not increase the salary from £7,956 to £10,000 to use up the director/shareholder's income tax personal allowance? Because the extra £2,044 of salary will attract both employee's and employer's national insurance, at 12% and 13.8% respectively:

Extra national insurance

£2,044 x 12%	£245
£2,044 x 13.8%	£282
Total	£527

On the plus side, the extra salary and employer's national insurance will attract corporation tax relief at 20%:

Extra corporation tax relief

£2,044 x 20%	£409
£282 x 20%	£56
Total	£465

The extra national insurance cost outweighs the extra corporation tax relief, so further salary beyond £7,956 is not, strictly speaking, 'optimal' (although there may be other reasons why a higher salary is desirable).

However, the extra tax cost is not significant (around £60), so whether you take a salary of £7,956, £10,000, or something in between, probably won't make a huge amount of difference at the end of the day.

Some company owners may wish to pay themselves a salary of £10,000 because, although strictly speaking not 'optimal', this lets them take a bigger chunk of income out of the company on a regular basis, without some of the hassle that comes with paying dividends (for example, making sure the company has sufficient distributable profits and that dividends are properly declared).

This juggling act gets to the heart of the salary/dividend question: as a company director/shareholder you have to compare the tax cost to you *personally* with the tax cost and tax relief enjoyed by your *company*.

In summary, for the 2014/15 tax year the most tax-efficient strategy for company owners with employees (i.e. no spare employment allowance) is to take a salary of £7,956. However, a salary of £10,000 can be taken with very little additional tax cost (around £60).

Company Profits over £300,000

Companies with profits over £300,000 currently face a higher corporation tax rate. The flipside is they get more corporation tax relief on their expenses, e.g. salaries. This raises the question: Is it tax efficient for directors of these companies to take a salary of £10,000 instead of £7,956?

This was certainly the case last year when corporation tax relief was available at 23.75%, even more so a few years ago when the top corporation tax rate was 29.75%. However, for the current financial year, the corporation tax rate applying to profits over £300,000 is just 21.25%.

Thus, the corporation tax relief on an additional £2,044 of salary and £282 of employer's national insurance comes to just £494 (£2,326 x 21.25%). This does not cover the extra national insurance cost of £527. In other words, a salary of £10,000 is not as tax efficient as a salary of £7,956.

However, the extra tax cost is insignificant (just over £30), so whether you take a salary of £7,956 or £10,000 probably doesn't make much difference at the end of the day.

In summary, for the 2014/15 tax year the most tax-efficient strategy for company owners with profits of more than £300,000 is to take a salary of £7,956 but £10,000 can be paid in most cases with very little extra tax cost.

How Much Salary?
Companies with No Employees
(i.e. with spare employment allowance)

In this section we'll take a look at companies that do NOT use up their £2,000 employment allowance paying salaries to other employees, i.e. there is spare employment allowance for the directors own salaries.

This group includes companies with no employees (e.g. one-man band companies) and companies with just a few low-paid employees.

Directors of these companies can pay themselves salaries of more than £7,956 without having to worry about *employer's* national insurance.

The question is, should they?

Salary of £10,000?

If a company owner increases his salary from £7,956 to £10,000 no national insurance will be paid by the company itself but the extra salary will result in a national insurance bill of £245 for the director personally (£2,044 x 12%). That's the bad news.

The good news is that, by increasing the director's salary from £7,956 to £10,000, at least £409 of additional corporation tax relief is obtained for the company (£2,044 x 20%).

The extra corporation tax relief outweighs the national insurance cost by £164 in the average small company.

In summary, for company owners with no employees (i.e. spare employment allowance), a salary of up to £10,000 will be more tax efficient than a salary of £7,956.

Salary over £10,000?

A company with no employees and only one director can pay that director a salary of up to £22,449 with no employer's national insurance.

A company with no employees and two directors (e.g. a husband and wife) can pay the directors a salary of up to £15,202 each with no employer's national insurance.

But is it worth paying salaries of more than £10,000 to avoid wasting the £2,000 employment allowance? In most cases the answer is no because any additional salary will also be subject to income tax. The 20% income tax and 12% national insurance paid by the directors outweighs the corporation tax relief (at 20% or possibly 21.25%) enjoyed by the company.

In summary, for the 2014/15 tax year the most tax efficient salary for company owners with no employees (i.e. companies with spare employment allowance) is £10,000.

A director who takes a £10,000 salary will receive £9,755 after tax (£10,000 less £245 national insurance).

Is a Lower Salary Preferable?

Although a salary of £10,000 may be 'optimal' for company owners with spare employment allowance, a lower salary may be preferable in some cases.

For example, if the company doesn't have any other employees, the directors may decide to pay themselves a salary of £7,956 each to avoid the hassle of having to make any national insurance payments (for example, to avoid late payment penalties).

Although a salary of £7,956 is completely tax free, it still has to be reported to HMRC as part of the normal payroll process (although it may be possible to make a single annual payroll submission in some circumstances – see Chapter 29).

As we shall see in Part 4, a lower salary may also be desirable when the director has income from other sources.

Higher Salaries

Finally, although the salaries discussed in this chapter are 'optimal' from a strict comparison of tax rates and thresholds, there may be other tax and non-tax reasons why you may wish to pay yourself a higher salary (see part 8).

Chapter 7

Salaries: Pension Benefits

Apart from being tax efficient a salary confers two extra benefits on the director/shareholder:

- State pension entitlement
- Ability to make private pension contributions

State Pension Entitlement

To protect your state pension entitlement you should pay yourself a salary that is greater than the national insurance 'lower earnings limit'.

For 2014/15, the lower earnings limit is £111 per week which requires a total annual salary of at least £5,772.

As we shall see in Chapter 16 it is sometimes more tax efficient for the director/shareholder to take a salary lower than the amounts outlined in the previous chapter.

However, if you want to protect your state pension entitlement, a salary of at least £5,772 should be paid in 2014/15 in preference to taking dividends.

Private Pension Contributions

Everyone under the age of 75 can make a pension contribution of £3,600 per year. The actual cash contribution would be £2,880, with the taxman adding £720 to bring the total gross contribution to £3,600.

If you want to make bigger pension contributions the contributions you make *personally* (as opposed to contributions made by your company) must not exceed your 'relevant UK earnings'. Salaries count as earnings; dividends do not.

For a company director taking the 'optimal' tax-free salary of £7,956, the maximum pension contribution he can make is £7,956.

This is the maximum *gross* contribution. The director would personally invest £6,365 (£7,956 x 0.8) and the taxman will top this up with £1,591 of basic-rate tax relief for a gross contribution of £7,956.

Similarly, a director taking a salary of £10,000 can make a maximum pension contribution of £10,000. The director would personally invest £8,000 (£10,000 x 0.8) and the taxman will top this up with £2,000 of basic-rate tax relief for a gross contribution of £10,000.

Directors who want to make bigger pension contributions have two choices:

- Pay themselves a bigger salary (i.e. more earnings)
- Get the company to make the pension contributions

(See Chapter 24 for more information on pension contributions.)

Chapter 8

Tax-free Dividends

If a director/shareholder needs more income than the small 'optimal' salary, as most probably will, the most tax-efficient solution is generally to take a dividend.

We know from Chapter 3 that dividends attract no national insurance and are free from income tax, providing the director is not a higher-rate taxpayer.

For the 2014/15 tax year you become a higher-rate taxpayer when your income exceeds £41,865, so as long as your total income is less than this you will not pay any income tax on your dividends.

Companies with Employees
(i.e. with no spare employment allowance)

A director/shareholder who takes a tax-free salary of £7,956 and has no other income can take a tax-free dividend of £33,909. Total income: £41,865.

Note, however, that this is the maximum *gross* dividend that can be extracted tax free (see Chapter 3 for an explanation of gross dividends).

The maximum *cash* dividend that can actually be paid out from the company's bank account is £30,518 (£33,909 x 0.9).

Combined with the tax-free salary, this gives the director/shareholder the maximum total tax-free income for 2014/15: £38,474:

- £7,956   tax-free salary
- £30,518   tax-free dividend

The Corporation Tax Bill

Although a cash dividend of £30,518 can be paid with no tax consequences for the director/shareholder, the payment is not completely tax free.

As we know, dividends are paid out of a company's after-tax profits. So for a company that has paid 20% corporation tax, a dividend of £30,518 will have resulted in a corporation tax bill of £7,630:

Pre-tax profits	£38,148
Less: corporation tax @ 20%	£7,630
After-tax profits/dividend	£30,518

So while dividends are tax efficient they are NOT tax free.

This is an important point to remember, especially if you want to grow your business rather than extract income from it.

If, for example, a small company incurs £38,148 of tax deductible expenditure before the end of its accounting period, its corporation tax bill will be reduced by £7,630. This will leave less after-tax profit to distribute as dividends but such a strategy may appeal to some business owners who would prefer to re-invest profits and minimise all taxes, including corporation tax.

The fact that dividends come with a corporation tax bill is also the reason why company owners should consider other profit extraction strategies, for example company pension contributions (Chapter 24).

Some non-cash payments like these are both tax free in the hands of the director/shareholder and provide corporation tax relief. This is the best case scenario when it comes to extracting money from your company.

Having said this, the fact remains that most company owners need to extract *cash* from their companies every year to cover their living costs.

This means some tax will usually always be payable, either by the company or the director personally. The key is to minimise it.

Salary vs Dividends

Although dividends are not completely tax free, they are still much more tax efficient than taking a bigger salary in the circumstances described so far.

We know from the preceding paragraphs that putting an additional £30,518 tax free in the hands of the director will result in a corporation tax bill of £7,630 (at 20%) but no other taxes.

To put an additional £30,518 of after-tax salary into the hands of the director/shareholder, an additional salary payment of £46,066 would be required, on top of the £7,956 salary already paid.

The combined income tax and national insurance on this extra salary comes to £21,905 (including up to £6,357 of employer's national insurance).

It's not quite as bad as it looks because the company can also claim corporation tax relief on the entire additional salary payment and the employer's national insurance. (Remember, as a company owner you are as concerned about your company's tax bill as your own personal tax bill.)

Total corporation tax relief on the extra salary would come to £10,485:

	£
Extra salary	46,066
Employer's national insurance	6,357
	52,423
Corporation tax relief @ 20%	10,485

The overall net tax cost of the extra salary comes to £11,420:

	£
Income tax and national insurance	21,905
Less: Corporation tax relief	10,485
Net tax cost	11,420

So by taking a £30,518 dividend instead of £46,066 of additional salary the director/shareholder will save a total of £3,790 tax:

	£
Net tax cost of salary	11,420
Less: Corporation tax dividend	7,630
	3,790

In summary, a dividend is not tax free but is more tax efficient than taking additional salary.

Companies with No Employees
(i.e. with spare employment allowance)

A director/shareholder with no other income who decides to take a salary of £10,000 (because the company has spare employment allowance or because the director simply wants a larger salary) can take a tax-free dividend of £31,865. Total income: £41,865.

This is the maximum *gross* dividend that can be extracted tax free. The maximum *cash* dividend is £28,679.

Combined with an after-tax salary of £9,755 (£10,000 less £245 employee's national insurance), this gives the director/shareholder a total income of £38,434 in 2014/15:

- £9,755   Salary
- £28,679   Tax-free dividend

Company Directors Tax Returns

Note that, even if you don't have any income tax to pay on your salary and dividends, you will still have to complete a tax return.

All company directors have this duty.

Chapter 9

Doubling Tax-free Income: Spouses & Partners

Many companies are started and run by married or unmarried couples.

For couples in business together, the salaries and tax-free dividends outlined in the previous two chapters can be doubled up.

In other words, where salaries of £7,956 are taken:

Tax-free salaries	£15,912
Tax-free dividends	£61,036
Total tax-free income	£76,948

Where salaries of £10,000 are taken (£9,755 after tax):

Salaries	£19,510
Tax-free dividends	£57,358
Total income	£76,868

For many couples the above amounts will be more than enough income to withdraw each year.

If we assume for the sake of simplicity that all income is paid out of current-year profits, salaries and dividends of £15,912 and £61,036 respectively imply that the company is making profits of at least £92,207.

Of course many company owners do not distribute all of the profits of the business and re-invest some to help the business grow.

Those couples that own more profitable companies or require more income than the above amounts face the prospect of paying income tax on any additional dividends withdrawn. We will return to them in Part 3.

Spouses/Partners Brought into the Business

Of course, not all companies are started or managed by couples. In some cases the business may have been started before the couple met. In other cases, one member of the couple may not want to become actively involved in the business, for example if they have their own career or do not work at all.

In these cases the questions from a tax planning perspective are:

- Can a spouse/partner be employed in the business?

- Can shares in the company be transferred to a spouse/partner?

- How much tax will the above two strategies save?

We will return to these important tax planning issues in Chapter 20.

Chapter 10

Maximising Tax-free Income

So far we have shown that a director/shareholder who takes a tax-free salary of £7,956 can extract a tax-free income of £38,474 in the current 2014/15 tax year.

A director/shareholder who takes a salary of £10,000 (e.g. because his company has spare employment allowance) can extract a tax-free dividend of £28,679 – total after-tax income £38,434.

The above amounts can be doubled up when the company is owned by a couple.

In this chapter we will take a look at how company owners can maximise their tax-free income.

Use it or Lose It!

A director/shareholder may decide to not withdraw the maximum tax-free income for several reasons:

- The company hasn't made sufficient profit
- The company doesn't have sufficient cash
- The company owner doesn't need the money

However, when it comes to tax-free income, it really is a case of use it or lose it: if you don't take the maximum tax-free amounts this year, you cannot take bigger tax-free amounts next year.

The Company Hasn't Made Sufficient Profit

The company doesn't need to have made any profit to pay *salaries* and tax-efficient salaries should be paid wherever possible because they are also a tax deductible expense and reduce the company's corporation tax bill (even if this is only at a later date if the company is currently not making profits). For example, a salary of £7,956 will reduce a small company's tax bill by £1,591.

Dividends, on the other hand, can only be declared if the company has sufficient distributable profits.

It is not necessary for the company to actually make a profit in the year the dividend is paid, as long as there are sufficient accumulated profits (after tax) from previous years.

(See Chapter 29 for more information.)

The Company Doesn't Have Sufficient Cash

Even if the company has made sufficient profits, there may not be enough cash inside the company to pay the maximum tax-free dividends, or the directors may wish to hold onto the company's cash to grow the business.

This does not necessarily mean that dividends should be reduced. Dividends can be declared and not paid immediately.

The unpaid amount will be credited to the director's loan account and a tax-free withdrawal can be made at some point in the future, when there is enough cash available in the company.

This may be more tax efficient than reducing dividends during one year and then declaring bigger *taxable* dividends in another year.

The Company Owner Doesn't Need the Money

There are many reasons why a company owner may not feel the need to withdraw the maximum amount of tax-free income from the company.

For example, the company owner may have other resources, such as inherited money or proceeds from selling another business or from selling other assets like property and shares. The company owner may also have a spouse/partner who earns enough income to support the family.

In these circumstances the company owner may believe it is prudent to preserve the company's cash by not withdrawing the maximum tax-free salary and dividend.

In reality, however, the company owner may simply be storing up an income tax problem for the future. If accumulated profits are eventually paid out as a large dividend, an income tax charge of 25% or 30.6% could be payable on a significant portion of any dividend declared.

If income is withdrawn on a more regular annual basis, even if not required immediately, income tax may be avoided altogether.

There is one important exception. If the director/shareholder has other taxable income from other sources, it may be prudent to take a smaller dividend.

So far we have been assuming that the director/shareholder has no other taxable income. If there is other taxable income that uses up the basic-rate band, then to avoid income tax it will be necessary to reduce dividends. (More about directors with other income in Part 4.)

Note that you can only have one 'allowance' of tax-free income per year, even if you own more than one company. For example, if you own two companies and have taken the maximum tax-free salary and dividend from one of them, you cannot take a second tax-free income from the second company.

Bumper Year, Frugal Dividends

If your company makes bigger than normal profits during one accounting period you may be tempted to pay yourself a bigger dividend, even if this results in income tax being payable on some of the dividend income.

Paying a bigger than normal dividend is perfectly acceptable from a tax planning perspective IF you expect the company's profits to remain at a higher level or continue to grow.

If, however, you expect the company's profits to fall back, it may be wiser to 'smooth' your income and withdraw any bumper profits gradually and free of income tax.

Example

Duncan and Kitty are equal owners of Dunkit Ltd. After paying tax-free salaries, the company is left with the following after-tax profits:

Year 1   £100,000
Year 2   £40,000
Year 3   £40,000

The couple prefer to extract all of the company's profits, rather than re-invest them in the business. To keep the example simple we will assume that a total tax-free dividend of £30,518 can be taken each year by each director/shareholder (£61,036 in total).

If all of the Year 1 profits are extracted as dividends during a single tax year, the couple may face a combined income tax charge of £9,741 (£100,000 - £61,036 = £38,964 x 25%).

Alternatively, Duncan and Kitty could hold back their 'surplus' profits of £38,964 and pay them out gradually over the next two tax years. Duncan and Kitty's dividend withdrawals will now be as follows:

Year 1   £61,036
Year 2   £40,000 + £21,036
Year 3   £40,000 + £17,928

Every year Duncan and Kitty's dividends are no greater than £30,518 each and there is therefore no income tax payable.

(Note that, in practice, the amount of tax-free dividends that can be withdrawn varies from one tax year to the next because of changes to the higher-rate threshold.)

Cash Rich, Profit Poor

Sometimes a company's profit and loss account may show a significant surplus and there may be a sizeable amount of cash in the company's bank account. This state of affairs will typically arise where the directors/shareholders have been prudent and only extracted some of the company's after-tax profits each year.

If the directors/shareholders expect the company's profits to decline (for example, because the owners of the business are gradually winding the company down with a view to retiring or because of adverse trading conditions), they could consider keeping dividend payments below the higher-rate threshold so that no income tax is payable on dividends.

Example

Gordon and Angela are equal owners of Ganges Garage Ltd. Over the last five years the company has made after-tax profits of £200,000 per year. Each year Gordon and Angela have taken a small tax-free salary and around £50,000 each in dividends. Each year the couple have paid several thousand pounds of income tax on their dividend income.

Because the couple did not extract all of the company's profits each year, there is now around £500,000 sitting in the company's bank account. The company's fortunes have changed dramatically thanks to competition from India and Gordon and Angela don't expect to make more than around £20,000 profit per year from now on. They're not that fussed and are quite happy to wind down the company gradually over the next few years, leaving them more time to spend with their grandchildren.

Gordon and Angela could now consider reducing their cash dividends from £50,000 to £30,518 each (2014/15 tax figures). By staying below the higher-rate threshold from now on, it may be possible to withdraw the profits accumulated in the company's bank account over a number of years with no income tax payable.

Windfall Receipts from Other Sources

If you have taxable income from another source or taxable capital gains, you may want to reduce the amount of income you withdraw from your company to *below* the tax-free amounts.

This may allow you to pay less income tax on your dividends or less capital gains tax.

This is especially the case if those other taxable receipts are *temporary* in nature, i.e. when they disappear you may be able to make bigger tax-free withdrawals from your company.

Part 3

How to Extract More Income Tax Efficiently

Chapter 11

Withdrawing More Income:
The £100,000 Threshold

Summary So Far

So far we have shown that a director/shareholder who takes a tax-free salary of £7,956 can extract a tax-free dividend of £30,518 for a total tax-free income of £38,474 in 2014/15. A director/shareholder who takes a salary of £10,000 (£9,755 after tax) can extract a tax-free dividend of £28,679 – total after-tax income £38,434.

In both scenarios the director/shareholder ends up with a salary plus *gross* dividends totalling £41,865 and is on the cusp of being a higher-rate taxpayer.

These amounts can be doubled in the case of companies owned and run by couples.

If you do not, on average, require more income than the tax-free amounts, you may be able to adopt an 'income smoothing' strategy – taking the maximum tax-free income every year where possible, regardless of whether the company has made bigger than normal profits or lower than normal profits.

Taking Bigger Dividends

If you want more income than the tax-free amounts, the optimal strategy is to take additional dividends, not salary, in order to avoid the extortionate national insurance payable on employment income. However, now that you have reached the higher-rate threshold you will pay 25% income tax on additional cash dividends.

The next two income tax thresholds you have to watch out for are:

- £50,000   Child benefit tax charge
- £100,000   Personal allowance withdrawal

In this chapter we will assume that the director/shareholder (or their spouse/partner) is not claiming any child benefit. We will return to child benefit in the next chapter.

In the absence of any child benefit being claimed, the next threshold most company owners have to watch out for is £100,000, where the income tax personal allowance starts to be withdrawn.

The standard personal allowance currently saves a higher-rate taxpayer up to £4,000 in income tax and many company owners will want to keep their income below £100,000 to avoid losing it.

Maximum Income Taxed at 25%

With total gross income of £41,865 the director/shareholder can take additional *gross* dividends of up to £58,135 before the £100,000 threshold is reached.

This means an additional cash dividend of up to £52,322 can be taken. The total income tax charge will be 25%, producing a total income tax bill of £13,081:

£58,135 gross dividend x 0.9 = £52,322 cash dividend

£52,322 x 25% = £13,081 income tax

A director/shareholder with a salary of £7,956 who wants to extract the maximum amount taxed at just 25% will be left with total after-tax income of £77,715:

£38,474 tax free + £52,322 - £13,081 = £77,715

A director/shareholder with a salary of £10,000 will be left with a total after-tax income of £77,675:

£38,434 + £52,322 - £13,081 = £77,675

Don't Forget the Corporation Tax Bill

It's tempting to think that a director/shareholder taking any of the amounts listed above is paying relatively little tax. In the case of company owners with salaries of £7,956, a total of £90,796 can be taken out (£38,474 + £52,322), with a total income tax bill of just £13,081. The effective tax rate is just 14%!

However, it's important to remember that, although the director's salary is a tax deductible expense for the company, dividends are always paid out of a company's profits *after tax*.

A company owner who withdraws the maximum income taxable at 25% will be in receipt of a cash dividend of £82,840. The corporation tax bill attached to such a dividend is £20,710 (if the company paid 20% tax on its profits).

Doubling Up

If the company is owned and managed by a couple, the income taxed at just 25% can potentially be doubled up.

In the case of company owners taking a salary of £7,956, the total after-tax income of the couple will be £155,430 and they will pay income tax of £26,162.

In the case of company owners taking a salary of £10,000, the total after-tax income of the couple will be £155,350 and they will pay income tax of £26,162 and national insurance of £490.

Income between £41,865 and £100,000
Salary of £7,956

Most small company owners who withdraw dividends greater than the tax-free amounts, will probably withdraw less than £100,000 in total from their companies. In other words, they will withdraw a salary and *gross* dividends of between £41,865 and £100,000.

Some sample income tax bills for these company owners are listed in Table 2a. It is assumed that a tax-free salary of £7,956 is taken.

TABLE 2a
Income between £41,865 and £100,000
Salary £7,956

Cash Income £	Income Tax £	After-tax Income £
38,474	0	38,474
40,000	382	39,619
45,000	1,632	43,369
50,000	2,882	47,119
55,000	4,132	50,869
60,000	5,382	54,619
65,000	6,632	58,369
70,000	7,882	62,118
75,000	9,132	65,869
80,000	10,382	69,619
85,000	11,632	73,369
90,000	12,882	77,119
90,796	13,081	77,715

Notes:
1. Salary of £7,956 taken with rest of income as dividends
2. Tax-free cash dividend £30,518
3. 25% income tax payable on additional cash dividends
4. Table contains small rounding errors

The incomes listed in Table 2a are made up of salary and *cash* dividends.

If you want to withdraw, say, £70,000 you can take a tax-free salary of £7,956 and a dividend of £30,518 for a total of £38,474. The additional cash dividend of £31,526 will result in a 25% income tax charge (£7,882). Total after-tax income: £62,118.

In all cases the amounts listed in Table 2 can be doubled for companies owned and run by couples. For example, a couple can withdraw £80,000 (£40,000 each) with a total income tax bill of £764 (£382 each).

TABLE 2b
Income between £41,865 and £100,000
Salary £10,000

Cash Income £	Tax £	After-tax Income £
38,679	245	38,434
40,000	575	39,425
45,000	1,825	43,175
50,000	3,075	46,925
55,000	4,325	50,675
60,000	5,575	54,425
65,000	6,825	58,175
70,000	8,075	61,925
75,000	9,325	65,675
80,000	10,575	69,425
85,000	11,825	73,175
90,000	13,075	76,925
91,000	13,325	77,675

Assumptions:
1. Salary of £10,000 (£9,755 net) with rest of income as dividends
2. Tax-free cash dividend £28,679
3. 25% income tax payable on additional cash dividends
4. Tax column includes £245 employee's national insurance

Income between £41,865 and £100,000
Salary of £10,000

Table 2b shows how much tax is payable by company owners who take a salary of £10,000, a tax-free cash dividend of £28,679 plus an additional amount of taxed dividend income.

If you want to withdraw, say, £70,000 you can take a salary of £10,000 (£9,755 net of employee's national insurance) and a tax-free cash dividend of £28,679 for a total after-tax income of £38,434. The additional cash dividend of £31,321 will result in a 25% income tax charge (£7,830). Total after-tax income: £61,925.

£7,956 versus £10,000 Salary

Before we move on, it's worth making one additional point for company owners who take salaries of £10,000.

In Chapter 6 it was stated that, where the company has spare employment allowance, an additional saving of £164 per director/shareholder can be obtained by increasing salaries from £7,956 to £10,000.

However, where the director/shareholders are higher-rate taxpayers and therefore pay tax on some of their dividend income, the saving is slightly smaller – around £112.

This is because of the peculiar way in which tax on dividends is calculated. If a director/shareholder's salary increases by £2,044, the amount of after-tax profit available for distribution as dividends falls by £1,635, so his gross dividend income falls by just £1,817.

In other words, the director/shareholder's total taxable income will go up by £227 (£2,044 - £1,817). If he is a higher-rate taxpayer, he will pay an additional £51 tax on the additional dividend income (£227 x 22.5%)

Although the additional tax is small the point worth noting is this:

Although a salary of £10,000 is more tax efficient than a salary of £7,956 if the company has spare employment allowance, the additional saving is not significant: £164 in most small companies where the director/shareholders are basic-rate taxpayers and just £112 where they are higher-rate taxpayers.

Chapter 12

How to Protect Your Child Benefit

If you want to withdraw more than the tax-free amounts from your company *and* your household receives child benefit, the next income tax bracket you have to be aware of is £50,000-£60,000.

Child benefit is gradually withdrawn where any member of a household has over £50,000 income. This is done by imposing a High Income Child Benefit Charge on the highest earner in the household.

Once the highest earner's income reaches £60,000, all of the child benefit will effectively have been taken away in higher tax charges.

The £50,000 threshold can be increased or decreased by the Government but does not automatically increase with inflation. In other words, over time more and more taxpayers will end up paying the new child benefit tax charge.

The child benefit charge has important implications for company owners who want to determine how much income to withdraw from their companies during the current and future tax years.

Child Benefit: How Much is it Worth?

Child benefit is an extremely valuable *tax-free* handout from the Government. Parents who qualify currently receive:

- £1,066 for the first child
- £704.60 for each subsequent child

Depending on the number of children, a family can expect to receive the following total child benefit payment:

Children	Total Child Benefit
1	£1,066
2	£1,771
3	£2,475
4	£3,180

plus £704.60 for each additional child

How Long Do Child Benefit Payments Continue?

Child benefit generally continues to be paid until your children are 16 years old.

The payments will continue until age 20 if the child is enrolled in full-time 'non-advanced' education, including:

- GCSEs
- A levels
- Scottish highers
- NVQ/SVQ level 1, 2 or 3
- BTEC National Diploma, National Certificate, 1st Diploma

So if your child is 16, 17, 18 or 19 and enrolled in one of the above courses, child benefit will continue to be paid.

Once the child is 20 years old all child benefit payments will cease.

The following courses do NOT qualify:

- Degrees
- Diploma of Higher Education
- NVQ level 4 or above
- HNCs or HNDs
- Teacher training

In other words, if your children are 16, 17, 18 or 19 and enrolled in any these courses, you will not receive any child benefit.

Total Value of Child Benefit

Child benefit payments continue for between 16 and 20 years. Based on current child benefit rates, the total amount you can expect to receive over the total period your child qualifies is:

- £17,056 to £21,320 tax free for the first child
- £11,274 to £14,092 tax free for each additional child

These are very much 'back of the envelope' figures because they ignore the potential danger that child benefit may not be increased in line with inflation in the years ahead.

However, they clearly illustrate how valuable child benefit is over many years and why it is worth protecting where possible.

The £50,000 Threshold for Company Owners

As in previous chapters, we have to distinguish between gross dividends and cash dividends. To avoid the child benefit charge you have to keep your salary and *gross* dividends below £50,000.

In previous chapters we have shown that company owners can take a total tax-free income comprising salary and gross dividends of £41,865.

This leaves you scope to pay an additional gross dividend of £8,135 (i.e. an additional cash dividend of £7,321) before the child benefit charge comes into force.

The total income tax payable on the additional dividend will be £1,830 (£7,321 x 25%).

Salary of £7,956

A company owner who takes a salary of £7,956 and wants to avoid the child benefit charge in 2014/15 can take a tax-free salary and dividend of £38,474 plus an additional taxable cash dividend of £7,321. Total *after-tax* income: £43,965.

For a company owned and managed by a couple, the above amounts can be doubled up. Total after-tax income: £87,930.

Salary of £10,000

A company owner who takes a salary of £10,000 and wants to avoid the child benefit charge in 2014/15 can receive a salary and tax-free dividend of £38,434 (net of £245 employee's national insurance) plus an additional taxable cash dividend of £7,321. Total *after-tax* income: £43,925.

For a company owned and managed by a couple, the above amounts can be doubled up. Total after-tax income: £87,850.

Income between £50,000 and £60,000

If you want to extract more income from your company you will face paying the High Income Child Benefit Charge.

For every £100 of income over £50,000 a tax charge equivalent to 1% of the child benefit is levied on the highest earner in the household.

For example, if the highest earner in the household has income of £55,000, the tax charge will be equivalent to 50% of the child benefit claimed.

If the highest earner in the household has income of £60,000 or more, the tax charge will be 100% of the child benefit claimed.

For the highest earner in the household the child benefit charge will create the following marginal tax rates on dividend income in the £50,000-£60,000 tax bracket:

Children	Marginal Tax Rate on Cash Dividends
1	37%
2	45%
3	53%
4	60%

Plus 8% for each additional child.

Example

David, a company owner, has taken a salary and gross dividends totalling £50,000 so far in 2014/15. He is the highest earner in a household claiming child benefit for two children.

David decides to withdraw an additional gross dividend of £10,000. His total income will be £60,000 so he will face the maximum child benefit charge. The tax payable on the additional dividend is £4,021, calculated as follows:

£9,000 cash dividend x 25%	*£2,250*
£1,771 child benefit x 100%	*£1,771*
Total additional tax	*£4,021*

The effective tax rate on the additional £9,000 cash dividend is 45%.

Income between £60,000 and £100,000

If your income is at least £60,000 you will already be paying the maximum child benefit charge. Income between £60,000 and £100,000 does not incur any further child benefit charge.

Gross dividends between £60,000 and £100,000 will continue to be taxed at an effective income tax rate of 25% of the cash amount.

Once your income rises above £100,000 you face a fresh tax sting: withdrawal of the income tax personal allowance.

How to Avoid the Child Benefit Charge

Clearly taxpayers have an enormous incentive to escape the much higher tax rates that apply to dividends in the £50,000-£60,000 bracket.

Company owners may find it easier than other taxpayers to escape the child benefit charge because they can alter the amount of dividend income they receive each year. Some company owners may be able to avoid the new charge altogether by keeping their income below £50,000.

Others, including those who usually withdraw more than £60,000 each year, may be able to avoid the charge in some tax years but not others, or partly reduce the charge.

Company owners can also spread their income among family members, for example, by gifting shares in the business to their spouses (see Chapter 20).

For the current and future tax years, the following dividend strategies could be considered (figures quoted include gross dividends in each case):

Smooth Income

If the income you withdraw is currently somewhere between the higher-rate threshold (£41,865) and £50,000, and you expect your income to continue growing, you could consider extracting approximately £50,000 for several tax years, where possible.

This may mean you pay yourself more income than you need to begin with and less income than you need later on, but by doing so you may be able to avoid the child benefit charge completely for several years.

Roller-Coaster Income

If you plan to withdraw over £60,000 from 2014/15 onwards, you could consider taking big dividends during some tax years and smaller ones in other tax years.

For example, instead of taking £75,000 every year, consider taking £100,000 every second year, if possible, and £50,000 in the intervening years. This will allow you to avoid the child benefit charge every second year.

Similarly, a company owner who normally takes £60,000 every year could consider taking £70,000 in year 1 and £50,000 in year 2, where possible.

Austerity

If your taxable income is normally over £50,000, you could consider keeping your income below £50,000 for several years to avoid the child benefit charge.

For example, let's say you have three children and your taxable income is normally £60,000. If for the next three years you can afford to withdraw just £50,000, you may be able to protect over £7,000 of child benefit.

Other Issues

When paying yourself dividends that are smaller than normal or bigger than normal there may be lots of other issues to consider.

For example, you can only declare bigger dividends if the company has sufficient distributable profits.

If you postpone taking some of your dividends until a future tax year you may leave yourself exposed to any future increase in tax on company owners. Remember tax rules are constantly changing.

Chapter 13

Income over £100,000

Summary So Far

So far we have shown that a director/shareholder of a company that has no spare employment allowance can extract a tax-free salary of £7,956, a tax-free cash dividend of £30,518 and an additional cash dividend of up to £52,322 taxed at 25%. Total pre-tax income: £90,796. Total after-tax income: £77,715.

If the company has spare employment allowance, a salary of £10,000 can be taken with a total national insurance cost of just £245. On top of this, a tax-free cash dividend of £28,679 can be taken and an additional cash dividend of up to £52,322 taxed at 25%. Total pre-tax income: £91,000. Total after-tax income: £77,675.

The above amounts can be doubled up if the company is also owned and run by your spouse/partner.

If you or your spouse/partner are claiming child benefit, you may also have to watch out for the £50,000 threshold (see Chapter 12).

Income between £100,000 and £120,000

Many director/shareholders will be satisfied with a net after tax income of almost £78,000.

For those company owners who wish to extract more cash, a dividend is often the best option.

However, now you face an additional tax sting: withdrawal of the £10,000 income tax personal allowance.

This is because the director/shareholder at this point has a salary and gross dividend income of £100,000. (Remember all formal dividend tax calculations work with gross dividends, not cash dividends.)

Once your taxable income rises above £100,000, your personal allowance is gradually withdrawn. It is withdrawn at the rate of £1 for every £2 of additional income.

In other words, if you have income of £101,000 your personal allowance will be reduced by £500. Once your gross income reaches £120,000 you will have no personal allowance left at all.

Company owners with a salary and gross dividend income in the £100,000 to £120,000 bracket face paying income tax at an effective rate of between 37.5% and 46% on any additional cash dividends they withdraw.

Example

Annabel, a small company owner, has already taken a salary and <u>cash</u> dividends totalling £90,796. Her salary and <u>gross</u> dividends come to £100,000.

She decides to pays herself additional gross dividend income of £1,000 (cash dividend £900). On the additional £1,000 gross dividend she will pay 22.5% income tax: £225.

She will also lose £500 of her personal allowance which means £500 of dividends that would have been tax free will now be taxed at 22.5%. Additional tax: £112.50. Her £7,956 salary is still tax-free and fully covered by her remaining personal allowance.

The total additional income tax is £337.50 which is equivalent to 37.5% of the £900 cash dividend.

Example revisited

Let's say Annabel pays herself additional gross dividend income of £20,000 (cash dividend £18,000).

On the additional £20,000 gross dividend she will pay 22.5% income tax: £4,500. She will also lose all of her personal allowance which means her salary of £7,956 will now be taxed at 20%. Additional tax: £1,591.

In addition, £2,044 of gross dividend income, previously covered by her personal allowance, will be taxed at 22.5%. Additional tax: £460.

Finally, her salary uses up £7,956 of her basic-rate band which means £7,956 of gross dividends will no longer be tax free and will be taxed at 22.5%. Additional tax: £1,790.

The total additional income tax is £8,341 which is equivalent to 46% of the £18,000 cash dividend.

Income between £120,000 and £150,000

The 37.5% and 46% tax rates do not apply to all dividend income over £100,000 – only income between £100,000 and £120,000.

Once your income exceeds £120,000 your personal allowance will have disappeared altogether and any additional dividends will be taxed at the regular rate applying to higher-rate taxpayers: 25% on cash dividends or 22.5% on gross dividends.

After that, the next threshold you have to watch out for is £150,000 where the additional rate of tax kicks in (see Chapter 14).

How to Avoid 47% Tax

Unlike regular salaried employees or owners of unincorporated businesses (sole traders and partnerships), company owners can avoid these extortionate tax rates by simply not paying themselves salary and gross dividends in excess of £100,000 per year.

In other words, a company owner taking a salary of £7,956 should extract cash dividends not exceeding £82,840 and a company owner taking a salary of £10,000 should extract cash dividends not exceeding £81,000.

A company owner whose income may fluctuate from year to year, in line with the company's profits, may want to consider smoothing income to avoid the £100,000 threshold. In other words, if possible try not to pay yourself a salary and gross dividends of £80,000 in year 1 and £120,000 in year 2. It may be better to pay yourself £100,000 during both tax years, to preserve your income tax personal allowance in year 2.

Bigger Companies

Owners of company's earning substantial profits face a dilemma. While they may choose to extract no more than £100,000 per year, ultimately they may end up with a lot of surplus cash inside their companies.

For example, if you are the only shareholder in a company that is making an after-tax profit of £200,000 per year, you may not wish to extract just £100,000 per year indefinitely, especially if the surplus cash is not needed to help grow the business.

Company owners who wish to pay themselves more than £100,000 per year may be able to occasionally preserve their personal allowances by adopting the 'roller-coaster' strategy: paying bigger dividends in some tax years and smaller dividends in other tax years.

Remember, once your income exceeds £120,000 your personal allowance will have disappeared altogether and there is no additional penalty for taking additional dividend income, providing you keep your income below £150,000.

For example, let's say you normally withdraw a salary of £7,956 and gross dividends which together total £120,000 per year. With this level of income you will enjoy no income tax personal allowance.

If instead you pay yourself income of £100,000 in year 1 and £140,000 in year 2, this will allow you to preserve your personal allowance in year 1. Potential tax saving: £3,841 (2014/15 tax rates).

Salary vs Dividends

If you have already taken a salary and gross dividends up to £100,000 and want to extract more money from your company then a dividend is usually the best option.

However, if you have not taken any salary out of your company during the current tax year, and want to extract more than £100,000, it *may* be possible to achieve additional tax savings by paying yourself a smaller salary or no salary at all.

The potential tax savings depend on a number of factors, including the level of the director/shareholder's income and whether the company has spare national insurance employment allowance.

For example, in Chapter 6 it was shown that, where a company has spare employment allowance, the optimal salary for most company owners is £10,000. However, where a company owner's taxable income exceeds £120,000 (i.e. he has no personal allowance), a tax saving of around £300 can be achieved by taking a salary equal to the £7,956 national insurance threshold instead. It may be possible to achieve further tax savings by reducing the salary even further.

Where the same company owner's taxable income lies somewhere between £100,000 and £120,000 (i.e. the band of income where the personal allowance is gradually withdrawn), it is also possible to save tax by taking a salary of £7,956 instead of £10,000 but the size of the saving varies from case to case. At some income levels the company owner's overall tax bill will actually *increase* significantly if he reduces his salary too much.

Companies with Employees

In Chapter 6 it was also shown that, where a company has employees and therefore does not have any spare employment allowance, the optimal salary for most company owners is £7,956. However, where a company owner's taxable income exceeds £120,000 (i.e. he has no personal allowance), a tax saving can be achieved by taking a smaller salary. However, the tax saving is not very impressive (less than £200 in most cases, which is a very small saving for someone with so much income).

Where the same company owner's taxable income lies somewhere between £100,000 and £120,000, it is also possible to save a bit of tax by reducing the salary below £7,956 but the savings vary from case to case. At some income levels the company owner's overall tax bill will increase significantly (by over £1,000) if he reduces his salary too much.

When You Should Not Reduce Your Salary

There are also various tax and non-tax reasons why you may not want to reduce your salary. In other words, what may be 'mathematically optimal' does not always make for sound tax planning.

Pensions are a case in point. Anyone who wants to make a pension contribution higher than £3,600 (the minimum contribution that can be made by anyone under age 75) requires earnings. Salaries count as earnings, dividends do not.

Furthermore, in order to protect your state pension entitlement, you should always make sure you receive a salary that exceeds the national insurance 'lower earnings limit'. For 2014/15, the lower earnings limit is £111 per week which requires a total annual salary of at least £5,772.

When it comes to reducing your salary to achieve additional tax savings the permutations are too many to provide any simple guidelines here. Any analysis would have to be performed on a case by case basis.

Chapter 14

Income over £150,000

Once your income rises above £150,000 you become an 'additional rate' taxpayer. Most people are familiar with the 45% tax rate (previously 50%) that applies to most types of income above this threshold.

However, if you are a company owner it is likely that it will be your dividend income that takes you over the £150,000 threshold (dividends are always treated as the top slice of income – see Chapter 15).

Once your dividend income rises above £150,000, the effective income tax rate rises from 25% to 30.6%. This is the rate applying to cash dividends.

However, as always, it is the amount of your *gross dividends* that will determine whether the £150,000 threshold has been breached.

The income tax rate applying to gross dividends over £150,000 is 37.5%. When you deduct the 10% notional tax credit the effective tax rate is 27.5%.

In summary, the effective tax rates applying to dividend income above £150,000 are as follows:

- Cash dividends – 30.6%
- Gross dividends – 27.5%

To avoid accidentally going over the £150,000 threshold, it is important to remember the difference between cash dividends and gross dividends.

Example

Helga is a company owner. During the current tax year she has salary income and rental income of £20,000. Her company has also paid her a cash dividend of £80,000.

She wants to take an additional dividend of £50,000 to help finance the purchase of a new property and is under the impression that she will avoid paying 30.6% tax because her total receipts will be exactly £150,000.

However, Helga has forgotten the difference between gross dividends and cash dividends.

Her total income so far is actually £108,889, made up of £20,000 of employment and rental income and £88,889 of gross dividends (£80,000/0.9).

An additional £50,000 cash dividend equates to a gross dividend of £55,556, bringing her total income to £164,445. Helga will pay 27.5% tax on £14,445 of her gross dividend income.

How much additional dividend income can Helga take if she wants to avoid paying the additional rate of tax?

Before taking the additional dividend she has income of £108,889. This means she can take an additional gross dividend of £41,111 (£150,000 - £108,889).

This means she can take an additional cash dividend of £37,000 (£41,111 x 0.9).

To avoid paying the additional rate of tax Helga may want to consider extracting the additional funds over more than one tax year, keeping her total income below £150,000 per year.

Don't Forget the Corporation Tax Bill

Although 30.6% is a lot lower than the 45% rate most people associate with income over £150,000, we must not forget that dividends are paid out of profits that have already been subject to corporation tax.

For example, if a company pays £20 corporation tax on £100 of profit, that leaves £80 to distribute as dividends. If the director/shareholder then pays 30.6% income tax on the £80 distribution, the additional tax comes to £24. The total tax paid by the director and the company is £44 which is 44%.

Will the Additional Rate Be Changed?

The Government has stated that the additional rate of tax, introduced in the dying days of Gordon Brown's premiership, is "temporary".

However, when the reduction from 50% to 45% was announced in the 2012 Budget (36.1% to 30.6% for dividends), no date was given for a further reduction.

The Liberal Democrats have fiercely resisted calls from Conservative backbenchers to reduce the top rate further. Earlier this year, Chief Secretary to the Treasury Danny Alexander claimed that any further cut would only happen "over my dead body" while the party was in government.

Reducing taxes on high income earners is, of course, politically very difficult. If anything, the top tax rate could be increased back to 50%. The Labour Party has pledged to do this if they win the next election.

Were this to happen, company owners would hopefully have sufficient warning and be able to make bigger than normal dividend withdrawals before the tax increase took effect.

Alternative Profit Extraction Strategies

Many company owners may wish to keep their total income below £150,000 by adopting various alternative profit extraction strategies, including:

- Postponing dividends until the additional rate of tax is abolished (although this may never happen!)

- Gifting shares in the business to family members, including family members who are higher-rate taxpayers (see Part 6).

- Making personal or company pension contributions.

It is important to not take any steps that you will later regret if the additional rate of tax is either increased or abolished altogether.

Part 4

Company Owners with Income from Other Sources

Chapter 15

Keeping Income Below the Key Thresholds

Introduction

In Chapter 5 we explained why company owners, when deciding how much income to withdraw from their companies, need to be aware of the following income tax thresholds and brackets:

- Over £41,865   Higher rate tax
- £50,000-£60,000   Child benefit tax charge
- £100,000-£120,000   Personal allowance withdrawal
- Over £150,000   Additional rate of tax

If a company owner's total taxable income is less than £41,865, he will not pay any income tax on his dividends. Once his income exceeds £41,865, he starts paying tax at 25%.

However, income that falls into the final three tax brackets is taxed at much higher rates:

- £50,000-£60,000   37% to 60% or more
- £100,000-£120,000   37.5% to 46%
- Over £150,000   30.6%

(Note: these are the tax rates applying to cash dividends although the thresholds apply to gross dividends. The £50,000-£60,000 threshold only applies to households in receipt of child benefit.)

When trying to avoid these extortionate tax rates, you must remember to include any other taxable income you receive. If you have taxable income from other sources it may force your company income, in particular your dividend income, into a higher tax bracket.

To avoid a potential tax sting you may wish to reduce the amount of income you withdraw from your company or take other steps to reduce your tax bill.

The Order in which Income is Taxed

Income is taxed in the following order:

- Non-savings income:
  - ➤ Employment income
  - ➤ Self-employment income
  - ➤ Rental income
- Savings income
- Dividend income

Dividends are always treated as the top slice of income.

Let's say you expect to earn £10,000 of rental income during the current tax year but, so far, have not withdrawn any income from your company. As things stand, all of your rental income will be tax free, being covered by your income tax personal allowance.

Let's say you now decide to withdraw a salary of £7,956 and a cash dividend of £30,518 from your company (the 'tax-free' amounts discussed in Chapters 6 and 8).

The decision to take a salary means you now have £17,956 of non-savings income and your income tax bill will increase by £1,591:

£17,956 - £10,000 personal allowance = £7,956 x 20% = £1,591

Effectively, you've paid 20% tax on your salary.

And what about your supposedly 'tax-free' dividends?

Your non-savings income uses up £7,956 of your basic-rate band, which means £7,956 of your *gross* dividends (£7,160 of your cash dividends) will now be pushed into the higher-rate tax bracket.

As a result, your dividends will no longer be completely tax free. There will be an income tax bill of £1,790 (£7,160 x 25%).

Income from Other Sources

With the exception of self-employment income, it may be possible to extract all of the various types of income listed above from your own company: employment income, rental income, interest income, and dividend income.

We've already talked extensively about salaries (employment income) and dividends. If your company uses a property that you own personally (for example, an office or shop) it can also pay you rent; and if your company borrows money from you it can pay you interest.

In Chapter 23 we take a look at whether it is tax efficient to get your company to pay you rent and how much.

In this chapter the focus is on company owners who have income from *other sources* – i.e. income that does not come out of their own company.

More specifically, the focus is on company owners who have income from other sources that is subject to *income tax*.

Some income (e.g. most interest income and stock market dividends) can be sheltered from income tax inside an ISA or pension scheme.

It is even possible to shelter assets from income tax inside a company. Some property investors do this. Corporation tax will still be payable on any rental profits produced by the properties but the income tax position of the director/shareholder will be unaffected, unless those profits are extracted.

Most company owners have at least some taxable income from other sources but the amounts are often trivial and can, by and large, be ignored (e.g. a few pounds of bank interest).

Those company owners who do have a significant amount of taxable income from other sources, and cannot shelter it from income tax, may wish to reduce the amount of income they withdraw from their own companies, so as to avoid paying income tax at some of the extortionate rates listed at the beginning of this chapter.

Other Income – Control

One of the benefits of being a company owner is that you can to a great extent control how much income you withdraw from your business. This allows you to control your income tax bill from year to year.

Income from other sources is often less easy to control. For example, it may not be possible to shift it from one tax year into another tax year. You may be able to control the dividends declared by your own company but you cannot force the board of Vodafone to increase or lower its dividend!

Company owners who want to keep their taxable income just below any of the key income tax thresholds may therefore have to increase or decrease their *company income* – it may not always be possible to alter income from other sources.

Gross Dividends vs Cash Dividends

If you have income from other sources and want to ensure that your dividend income does not breach the £41,865, £50,000, £100,000, or £150,000 thresholds, it is critical to remember that it is your *gross* dividends that are relevant, not the cash dividends you receive from your company.

Example

Maria owns a small company and decides to pay herself a salary of £7,956. She also has rental profits of £10,000 from some buy-to-let properties. She wants to take a big dividend out of her company but does not want her taxable income to exceed £100,000, the point at which her personal allowance will be withdrawn.

How much dividend income can she withdraw? She already has income of £17,956, which means she can withdraw a gross dividend of £82,044 (£100,000 - £17,956). The maximum cash dividend she can withdraw is £73,840 (£82,044 x 0.9).

Table 3 shows the maximum cash dividend you can withdraw during 2014/15 if you have other taxable income (including employment income) and want to avoid some of the key income tax thresholds.

TABLE 3
Avoiding the Tax Thresholds
Maximum Cash Dividend 2014/15

Other Income	Threshold		
	£41,865	**£50,000**	**£100,000**
£7,956	£30,518	£37,840	£82,840
£10,000	£28,679	£36,000	£81,000
£15,000	£24,179	£31,500	£76,500
£20,000	£19,679	£27,000	£72,000
£25,000	£15,179	£22,500	£67,500
£30,000	£10,679	£18,000	£63,000
£35,000	£6,179	£13,500	£58,500
£40,000	£1,679	£9,000	£54,000
£45,000	£0	£4,500	£49,500
£50,000	£0	£0	£45,000

Note: Table may contain small rounding errors

For example, if you have other taxable income of £20,000 a cash dividend of £19,679 will keep your income below £41,865 and be completely tax free.

A cash dividend of up to £27,000 will ensure that your income does not exceed £50,000. Some of the dividend income will be taxable but you will avoid the child benefit tax charge.

A cash dividend of up to £72,000 will ensure that your income does not exceed £100,000. A significant amount of your dividend income will be taxed at 25% and you may end up paying the maximum child benefit tax charge but you will not lose any of your personal allowance.

Other Income –Predictability

At the start of a new tax year you may not know with complete certainty how much taxable income you will receive from other sources during the year.

This could be problematic if you wish to withdraw dividends from your company *at the beginning of the tax year* (see Chapter 18).

If you withdraw dividends from your company and your other income then turns out to be higher than expected, you may end up paying more income tax than you expected on your company dividends.

Some types of income are, however, more predictable than others. For example, interest income, stock market dividends and rental income are arguably more predictable than, say, the profits of a sole trader business (self-employment income).

Some types of income, if not completely predictable, are more likely to end up being *less than expected*, rather than higher than expected. For example, a rental property that normally generates rental income of £1,000 per month may lie empty for three months, thereby producing an annual income of £9,000 rather than £12,000.

If your income from other sources turns out to be less than expected, you may be able to get your company to pay you additional dividend income before the end of the tax year.

If your income from other sources turns out to be *higher than expected* you generally cannot reverse any dividends you have already taken out of your company, although it may be possible to do some emergency year-end tax planning (see below).

Company owners who have unpredictable income from other sources may therefore wish to postpone paying dividends until closer to the end of the tax year, if they are concerned that their dividend income may fall into a heavily taxed bracket.

Chapter 16

Should I Pay Myself a Smaller Salary?

So far we have shown that, if you have income from other sources, you may wish to reduce your company *dividends* to avoid various tax thresholds.

Another important question is: "Should I pay myself a smaller salary?"

In *theory*, your after-tax disposable income can be maximised by reducing your company salary.

How is the 'optimal' salary calculated? Generally speaking, by deducting your other income from your income tax personal allowance (£10,000 for 2014/15). For example, if you have rental income of £4,000, your optimal salary would be:

$$£10,000 - £4,000 = £6,000$$

In Chapter 6 it was shown that, where a company has spare national insurance employment allowance, the optimal salary for most company owners is £10,000.

However, where the company owner has taxable income from other sources, it may be possible to achieve a tax saving of several hundred pounds by taking a salary equal to the £7,956 national insurance threshold instead. It may also be possible to achieve additional tax savings by reducing the salary even further.

Companies with Employees

In Chapter 6 it was also shown that, where a company has employees and therefore does not have any spare employment allowance, the optimal salary for most company owners is £7,956.

However, where the company owner has taxable income from other sources, a tax saving can be achieved by taking a smaller salary. However, the increase in the company owner's after-tax disposable income may be very small (under £100).

I stated above that, in *theory*, it is optimal to reduce your salary. There are lots of reasons why you may not wish to reduce your salary or why it may not be practical to reduce it:

- To keep your earnings above the lower earnings limit (£5,772 in 2014/15) to protect your state pension entitlement (See Chapter 7).

- To make bigger pension contributions (see Chapter 24).

- Because your income from other sources may not be known at the beginning of the year, when you may wish to start making monthly salary payments.

- Because the taxman may question any reduction in your salary (see Chapter 31).

Chapter 17

The Different Types of Income

Let's take a closer look at the different types of income you may earn from other sources and how they may affect the income you decide to withdraw from your own company:

Employment Income

It is possible to have more than one source of employment income, for example:

- Salary from a second job with a separate employer, or
- Salary from a second company you own

If you have recently started out in business, it is possible that you will have a second job (possibly a part-time job) to help pay the bills.

If you start a second company to house a separate business venture there is, of course, nothing to stop you paying yourself a second salary.

For income tax purposes you are only entitled to one personal allowance (£10,000 in 2014/15). This generally means that you can only have one tax-free salary (unless, of course, the two salaries, when added together, total less than £10,000). Some or all of the second salary may be taxed at 20%.

National insurance is generally calculated differently. Employees who have more than one small salary (less than £7,956 in 2014/15), may not have to pay national insurance contributions at all. This is because the earnings from each job may be treated separately.

If the two businesses are in association, however, the salaries will be added together and national insurance may be payable.

Employers are considered to be in association if:

- The businesses serve a common purpose, and

- There is significant sharing of things like premises, personnel, equipment or customers

Is it a good idea to pay yourself two salaries IF both are exempt from national insurance? If your income tax personal allowance has not been fully utilised, it may be possible to increase your after-tax disposable income by a small amount (approximately £150) by paying yourself enough second salary to use up your remaining personal allowance.

Once your personal allowance has been fully utilised, a dividend may be more tax efficient than a second salary (or have the same overall tax cost).

There may, of course, be other tax and non-tax reasons why you wish to pay yourself a second salary or a bigger second salary.

Self-Employment Income

You may have self-employment income if you have another business and that business is not a company (i.e. you are a sole trader or belong to a partnership). Many entrepreneurs have multiple businesses and it's possible that a second or third business will not be run via a company.

Companies are wonderful tax shelters but unincorporated businesses have advantages of their own, including lower accountancy fees, more generous treatment of certain expenses and more generous capital allowances for cars used in the business.

Self-employment income may be difficult to predict – especially close to the beginning of a new tax year – making it difficult to decide how much income to withdraw from the other business that is housed in a company. Fortunately, when it comes to self-employment income, it is often possible to do some emergency year-end tax planning (e.g. by making pension contributions or buying items for the business that are tax deductible thanks to the annual investment allowance – see below).

Losses from Previous Tax Years

If you have a self-employment loss brought forward from earlier years it can be set off against any profits made in the current year.

If the loss is big enough, you will not have any *taxable* self-employment income in the current year. This means you will not have to worry about your self-employment income using up your personal allowance and basic-rate band, thereby pushing your company dividends into a higher tax bracket.

Rental Income

When we use the term 'rental income' what we mean is rental *profit*. You may receive rents of £10,000 per year but your rental profits may only be £5,000, after deducting mortgage interest, repairs and all the other tax deductions property investors can claim.

Unlike interest income and stock market dividends, most rental income cannot be sheltered from income tax in an ISA, pension scheme or other tax shelter.

There are, however a couple of exceptions:

- Commercial property held in a pension scheme

- Residential or commercial property held in a company

Some business owners place their trading premises inside a self-invested personal pension (SIPP) to avoid income tax and capital gains tax.

Others put their properties in a company. Corporation tax will still be payable but your own income tax bill will be unaffected, unless the property company's profits are extracted.

Apart from these two exceptions, most landlords own their properties *personally*, which means they are fully exposed to income tax on their rental profits. These rental profits may then need to be factored into the mix when deciding how much income you withdraw from your company.

Taxable Rental Profits

Some property investors have rental profits but do not have *taxable* rental profits.

If you have rental losses brought forward from previous years you will not have to pay any income tax on the rental profit you make during the current tax year (providing, the loss brought forward is big enough to completely offset the current year's profit).

Rental losses are common in practice. If the rental profit you make during the current tax year is not taxable it does not need to be factored into the mix when deciding how much income you withdraw from your company.

How Much Tax is Payable on Rental Profits?

A company owner with a small tax-free salary that uses up most of their income tax personal allowance could end up paying 20% tax on some or all of their rental income.

By using up some of the basic-rate band, the rental income could also push dividends into a higher tax bracket.

The potentially heavy tax bill attached to rental income is important to bear in mind if you are weighing up the pros and cons of investing in property, shares or other investments.

A higher-rate taxpayer who receives £5,000 of dividends from shares held in an ISA will pay no income tax. If the same individual receives £5,000 of rental income from buy-to-let property, income tax of £1,000 could be payable on the rental income itself (at 20%).

The rental income will also use up £5,000 of the individual's basic-rate band, which means £5,000 of *gross* dividend income (£4,500 of cash dividends) will now be pushed into the higher-rate tax bracket, producing an additional income tax bill of £1,125 (£4,500 x 25%).

Total tax on ISA dividends: 0%. Effective tax rate on rental income: 42.5%.

Interest Income

Many company directors will have some taxable bank account interest. However, these amounts will often be trivial because most interest income can (or *should*) be sheltered from tax inside an ISA or SIPP.

Other tax-free investments include index-linked savings certificates (when they're available) and offset mortgages (instead of earning interest, your savings are used to reduce the interest on your mortgage). Even paying off personal debts is effectively a way to earn tax-free interest.

Wealthier individuals, with large cash balances or holdings of corporate and government bonds may, of course, have a significant amount of taxable interest income and this income will need to be factored into the equation when they decide how much income to withdraw from their companies

There may also be times in life when you cannot avoid having significant amounts of taxable interest income:

- You sell your home and have a large cash lump sum
- You lend money to a friend or family member
- You receive a big dividend and put the cash in the bank
- You lend money to your company

10% Tax on Interest

When it comes to interest income, many company owners are in a fortunate position. They can have up to £2,880 of interest taxed at the 10% 'starting rate' (2014/15 figures).

Example 1

Mandy is a company director with a salary of £7,956 and interest income of £4,924. She has no other taxable income. There is no income tax or employee's national insurance on her salary. £2,044 of her interest income is covered by her remaining income tax personal allowance (£10,000 in 2014/15). The remaining £2,880 of her interest income is covered by the starting rate band and taxed at 10%.

The starting rate is supposed to benefit only those with very low incomes. Hence the £2,880 starting rate band is reduced by any other taxable *non-savings* income you have including:

- Employment income
- Self-employment income
- Pension income
- Rental income

If your taxable non-savings income exceeds the £2,880 starting rate band, none of your interest income will be taxed at 10%. It will then typically be taxed at 20%.

Example 2

The facts are exactly the same as Example 1 except Mandy also has £5,000 of rental income. £2,044 of her rental income is tax-free thanks to her remaining income tax personal allowance. The balance of £2,956 is Mandy's taxable non-savings income. Because Mandy's taxable non-savings income exceeds the £2,880 starting rate limit, none of her interest income is taxed at 10%. All of it is taxed at 20%.

Of course, most regular salary earners and self-employed business owners will have more than £2,880 of taxable non-savings income. Many company owners are in a different position, however. Note that the above list of non-savings income does NOT include dividends. Dividends are the top slice of income and do not use up the starting rate band.

Because company owners often pay themselves small salaries and take the rest of their income as dividends, they will often have little or no 'non-savings income'. As a result, they may not pay any more than 10% tax on their interest income.

Example 3

Mandy is a company director with a salary of £7,956, interest of £4,924 and dividends of £25,000. There is no income tax or national insurance on her salary. £2,044 of her interest income is covered by her income tax personal allowance. The remaining £2,880 of her interest income is taxed at 10%. All of her dividends are tax free because she is not a higher-rate taxpayer (her total income is less than £41,865).

Hence many company directors will pay no more than 10% tax on their interest income if:

- They take a small salary from their company,

- Do not have a sole trader or partnership business, and

- Rental income doesn't use up the £2,880 starting rate band.

The 10% tax rate could be useful to company directors who pay themselves a substantial cash dividend, perhaps at the start of the tax year. Unless they have an offset mortgage or invest the money immediately in an ISA or SIPP, they will pay income tax on any interest generated by their cash lump sum.

Higher-Rate Taxpayers

It is important to point out that the 10% starting rate band is not given in addition to the basic-rate band (£31,865 in 2014/15). Instead it is part of the basic-rate band.

In other words, if you qualify to use the starting rate band your basic-rate band will be reduced and this could push some of your dividend income into a higher tax bracket.

Example 4

Mandy is a company director with a salary of £7,956 and dividends of £30,518 (the tax-free amounts discussed in Chapters 6 and 8). She also has interest income of £4,924.

There is no income tax on her salary and £2,044 of her interest is covered by her personal allowance. The remaining £2,880 of her interest income is taxed at 10%. Total tax on interest income: £288.

Her basic-rate band is reduced by £2,880, which means £2,880 of her gross dividends (£2,592 of her cash dividends) will be subject to higher-rate tax. Total tax on dividend income: £648.

Total additional tax thanks to presence of interest income: £936.

You could argue that Mandy is not, in fact, paying 10% tax on her taxable interest income but 32.5%:

$$£936/£2,880 \ x \ 100 = 32.5\%$$

Future Changes to the Starting Rate

As one of the concessions to savers in the March 2014 Budget, it was announced that, from 2015/16, the starting rate will be reduced from 10% to 0% and the starting rate band will be increased from £2,880 to £5,000.

This means that company owners will be able to receive up to £5,000 of interest *tax free* each year.

However, it's important to remember that, if a company owner increases his interest income to take advantage of the new 0% starting rate band, this could push some of his dividend income into a higher tax bracket.

Stock Market Dividends

The big difference between dividends from your own company and dividends from stock market companies is that stock market dividends can be completely sheltered from income tax by investing via an ISA or SIPP.

In practice, many stock market investors do in fact end up with a mixture of shares held inside and outside the tax protection of ISAs and SIPPs. A good example is a cash-rich investor who wants to invest more than the new £15,000 ISA limit but doesn't want to put his money in a pension.

These investors could consider adopting the following strategy:

- Hold high-income shares inside an ISA (to protect the dividends from income tax), and

- Hold growth shares that produce capital gains outside an ISA (because up to £11,000 of capital gains will be tax free anyway thanks to the annual CGT exemption).

This strategy will not always produce the biggest tax savings, however. If you bought Apple shares back in 2003 – before their almost 10,000% rise – you would be kicking yourself if you didn't stick them in an ISA!

Stock Market Dividends – How Big a Problem?

Unlike dividends from your own company, you cannot control the amount of income you receive from stock market companies.

So if you have significant dividends from stock market companies, and the shares are not sheltered inside an ISA or SIPP, you may want to reduce the dividends you extract from your own company to avoid going over one of the key income tax thresholds.

However, my gut feeling is that stock market dividends do not cause tax problems for most individuals. The main exception is wealthy investors who hold a significant portfolio of shares outside a tax wrapper.

Even if you own, say, £100,000 worth of shares outside an ISA or SIPP you will probably receive no more than £4,000 per year in dividends, producing an income tax bill of £1,000 for a higher-rate taxpayer.

Short-term (Emergency) Tax Planning

If you find that your total taxable income is higher than expected, there are some steps you can take to reduce it before the end of the tax year:

Pension Contributions

Everyone under age 75 can make a gross pension contribution of £3,600 per year. The taxpayer personally contributes £2,880 and the taxman tops up the pension plan with £720 of basic-rate tax relief.

To make bigger pension contributions you require earnings: generally salary income or self-employment profits.

If you have a salary of £7,956 you can make a gross pension contribution of £7,956 (£6,365 from you, £1,591 from the taxman). Your basic-rate band will be increased by £7,956 so £7,956 of your gross dividends may escape higher-rate tax.

If you have self-employment income you can generally make an additional gross pension contribution equivalent to the taxable profits of the business, thereby eliminating any tax problem caused by this type of income.

See Chapter 24 for more information on pension contributions.

Tax Deductible Expenditure

Self-employed business owners (sole traders and partnerships) can also reduce their taxable income by incurring tax deductible expenditure before the end of the business's tax year.

Possibly the easiest way is to incur expenditure that qualifies for an immediate tax deduction thanks to the annual investment allowance. The annual investment allowance was increased from £250,000 to £500,000 in April 2014 and this increase will last until 31 December 2015, at which point it will fall back to £25,000.

Property investors with higher than expected rental profits can spend money on property repairs before the end of the tax year, e.g. replacement kitchens and bathrooms.

Long-term Tax Planning

Company owners with significant amounts of income from other sources may be able to take the following steps to shift income from themselves to another entity or person:

Self-Employment Income

Consider putting the business into a second company (company 2) so that corporation tax is payable rather than income tax. Dividends can then be extracted from company 2, taking into account dividends withdrawn from company 1. This will allow you to control your income tax bill from year to year.

Of course, it's not always advantageous to incorporate a second business. Sole traders and partnerships enjoy certain tax benefits, including more generous tax treatment of various expenses (including home office, travel and car capital allowances).

Rental Income

- Transferring properties to your spouse if he/she pays income tax at a lower rate.

- Holding commercial properties inside a pension scheme.

- Holding investment properties inside a company, so that corporation tax is payable instead of income tax and the extraction of rental profits (as dividends) can be controlled. See the Taxcafe guide *Using a Property Company to Save Tax* for a full discussion of the benefits and drawbacks of using a company.

- Consider alternative investments (e.g. blue chip shares) that can be sheltered from tax in an ISA or pension scheme.

Interest Income

- Transfer savings into an ISA or SIPP.

- Use savings to pay off debt or take out an offset mortgage.

- Transfer cash to certain family members who pay tax at a lower rate.

- Invest in assets that produce capital growth rather than interest income.

Stock Market Dividends

- Hold shares in an ISA or SIPP.

- Transfer holdings to a spouse and possibly other family members.

Part 5

Tax on Dividends: Minimising the Pain

Chapter 18

How to Postpone Paying Tax for 666 Days

In Chapters 6 and 8 we explained how company owners may be able to extract a tax-free salary of £7,956 and a tax-free cash dividend of £30,518 in 2014/15. The optimal amounts are generally £10,000 and £28,679 respectively, if your company has spare national insurance employment allowance.

If you want to extract more money from your company, the optimal strategy is normally to pay yourself additional dividends.

Income tax will generally be payable on any additional dividend income (normally at 25% of the cash amount) but, unlike additional salary, no national insurance is payable.

There are also *cash flow benefits* when it comes to paying yourself additional dividends. Unlike salaries and bonuses, on which income tax and national insurance is payable almost immediately, the income tax on dividends is generally not payable until the 31st of January following the end of the tax year.

In this chapter we will explain, with the help of a case study, how you may be able to postpone paying income tax on additional dividends by almost two years.

Case Study – Upping Dividends

Victor and his wife Ann are equal owners of Le Gourmand Ltd, a company that has built a reputation selling luxury imported foods to hotels, restaurants and delicatessens.

During the boom years the company made handsome profits. The couple extracted quite a lot of these profits as dividends but also kept a fair amount in the company, building a £200,000 cash buffer to tide them through the bad times.

During the worst of the recession the company's profits fell dramatically and Ann and Victor only withdrew enough dividends to use up their basic-rate tax bands (see Chapter 8).

In the last couple of years the company has taken off again, thanks to Ann's idea to start exporting caviar, truffles, and other luxury foods to Vietnam. The company is now sitting on a cash pile of £300,000.

During the 2014/15 tax year, starting on 6 April 2014, Victor and Ann would like to withdraw around £150,000 of this cash as dividends (£75,000 each), plus a tax-free salary of £7,956 each. (We will assume that the company has sufficient distributable profits to pay these dividends – see Chapter 29.)

The couple know they will have to pay income tax on some of their dividend income but they are very confident their business will continue to grow and generate even more cash, which they will eventually want to withdraw as well.

Although they could probably afford to withdraw even higher dividends, they want to keep a decent chunk of cash in the company to fund its Asian venture. They certainly don't want to see their taxable incomes go over the dreaded £100,000 level, which would see their income tax personal allowances withdrawn.

The Company's Cash

Victor is anxious to up their dividends as soon as possible because he is outraged at the interest the bank is paying on the company's cash (less than 1%).

He wants to take a big chunk of the couple's £150,000 cash dividend and invest it either in rental property or shares.

In fact, Victor reckons he may be able to generate sufficient returns on the invested money to cover the income tax they will have to pay on their dividends.

Alternatively, the couple may just take the low risk route and use the money taken out of the company to pay off some of the mortgage on their home (the bank is charging them 4% interest on that).

How Much Income Tax Will They Pay?

On 6 April 2014, the very first day of the new tax year, Ann and Victor declare and pay a cash dividend of £75,000 each – £150,000 in total.

£30,518 each of Ann and Victor's dividends will be tax free – £61,036 tax free in total.

The remaining £44,482 each of their cash dividends – £88,964 in total – will be taxed at 25%, resulting in a combined income tax bill of £22,241.

We will assume that there are no other adverse tax consequences: Victor and Ann don't have any other taxable income and are therefore not in danger of having income over the £100,000 level, which would see their personal allowances withdrawn, let alone the £150,000 threshold where 30.6% income tax is payable on cash dividends.

Now for the important part:

Although tax of £22,241 is payable, the bill is not due until 31 January after the end of the tax year – i.e. 31 January 2016!

To recap, they pay themselves dividends on 6 April 2014 and the income tax is only payable on 31 January 2016.

So, by paying themselves dividends at the very beginning of the tax year, Ann and Victor have managed to postpone their income tax bills by one year, nine months and 26 days – 666 days in total!

There is a saying in the tax advice business that the next best thing to avoiding tax altogether is deferring it.

The longer you can defer paying tax, the longer you have free use of the taxman's money, as we shall now see.

The High-Risk Strategy

To cover day-to-day living expenses, Ann and Victor have their small salaries and tax-free dividends. Their total tax-free income is £76,948.

They decide to invest their additional taxable dividends – £88,964 – in some stock market funds. Fortunately for the couple they enjoy capital growth of 25% over the period of almost two years.

By 31 January 2016 – the due date for the income tax on their dividends – their initial investment of £88,964 has grown in value to £111,205. Their total capital gains come to £22,241.

In summary, Ann and Victor have an income tax bill of £22,241 on their dividends but, because the tax bill was deferred for 666 days, they have had time to invest the money and enjoy capital gains of £22,241.

The couple have completely covered their income tax bills.

Paying the Income Tax Bill

If Ann and Victor don't have any other cash available on 31 January 2016, they may have to sell some of their investments to pay the income tax on their dividends.

In this instance it is likely that no capital gains tax will be payable on their stock market profits – their capital gains will be completely covered by their annual CGT exemptions (£11,100 per person in 2015/16).

To pay their income tax bills they may have to sell investments worth £22,241. This means they will realize capital gains of £4,448, well within the tax-free limits. How do we calculate £4,448? The couple's investments are worth £111,205 but only £22,241 of this is made up of capital gains (20%):

$$£22,241/£111,205 \times 100 = 20\%$$

So if the couple sell investments worth £22,241 to pay the income tax on their dividends, 20% of the proceeds will constitute capital gains:

$$£22,241 \times 20\% = £4,448$$

In summary, to pay the £22,241 income tax bill on their dividends the couple may have to sell investments and realize capital gains of £4,448 (£2,224 each). These capital gains should be tax free thanks to the couple's annual CGT exemptions.

It should also be pointed out that a significant portion of the couple's £88,964 initial investment capital can be sheltered from tax in ISAs during the period. At the very outset, on 6 April 2014, a total of £23,760 (£11,880 each) could be invested in ISAs plus a further £6,240 on 1 July (when the ISA limit is raised to £15,000), plus a similar amount on 6 April 2015.

In summary, two thirds of their investment capital can be sheltered from the taxman in just over one year, allowing them to earn tax-free returns on the money extracted from the company.

The Low Risk Strategy

Of course, there's a good reason why the above strategy is labelled 'high risk': Ann and Victor's investments could *fall* in value over the period. A similar risk of capital loss would also be faced if the money had been invested in rental property.

Most financial advisors would agree that you should only be investing in assets like shares and property if you have a long-term investment horizon.

For this reason, it may be more prudent for Ann and Victor to only invest some of their surplus cash in the stock market. They could take £22,241 – the amount of income tax owing – and stick it in a savings account. This way they know they will have the funds to pay their tax bills.

A lower risk alternative to investing in the stock market would be to use their £88,964 of taxable dividends to reduce the mortgage on their home.

This alternative strategy may be most attractive to those who have an offset mortgage or any other type of 'flexible mortgage'. These allow you to access the money used to reduce your mortgage debt, when the need arises.

How much mortgage interest will the couple save? At present, their mortgage interest rate is 4%. Not having to pay this interest for 666 days on £88,964 of debt will save the couple approximately £6,500 in mortgage interest.

In other words, the interest saved on their mortgage could pay off around 30% of the £22,241 income tax payable on their dividends.

Summary

In summary, if Ann and Victor pull off the higher-risk share investment strategy, they will completely cover the income tax payable on their dividends.

With the lower-risk mortgage strategy, they will have to pay out around £15,741 (£22,241 income tax less £6,500 mortgage interest saved over almost two years).

However, that's not a bad result when you stop to consider that their total income for the year is £165,912 (£150,000 in cash dividends plus £7,956 each in salaries). Their effective tax rate is just 9.5%!

Payments on Account

For the first time in several years, Ann and Victor may also face the prospect of having to make payments on account. It may be possible to avoid these, however, as we shall see in the next chapter.

Chapter 19

How to Avoid the Dreaded Payments on Account

If most of the tax you pay is not deducted at source (e.g. PAYE), then you may have to make payments on account under the self-assessment system.

Payments on account allow HMRC to collect some of the tax you owe early. The most common victims are sole traders, business partners, landlords with rental profits, and higher-rate taxpayer company directors.

For income earned during the current tax year, which started on 6 April 2014 and ends on 5 April 2015, income tax is normally due on 31 January 2016.

But, if you have to make payments on account, you will have to make two earlier payments:

- One by 31 January 2015
- One by 31 July 2015

Each payment is normally half the previous year's self assessment tax (i.e. your total tax bill for the year less any tax deducted at source).

Making payments on account is still much better than paying tax through the PAYE system. The first payment is only due ten months into the tax year and the second payment is only due approximately four months after the tax year has ended.

Nevertheless, payments on account give many business owners a serious cashflow headache. Before we look at how you can minimise the pain, it's important to explain who exactly has to make these early tax payments.

Who Has to Make Payments on Account?

Payments on account are all about the tax you paid in the *previous tax year*.

You only have to make payments on account if your self-assessment tax (i.e. ignoring tax deducted at source) for the previous tax year was more than £1,000.

You do not have to make payments on account, however, if more than 80% of your total tax from the previous year was covered by tax deducted at source.

No payments on account are due in respect of capital gains tax.

Case Study Continued

Remember Ann and Victor from the previous chapter? They face a combined income tax bill of £22,241 as a result of the dividends they are taking out of their company during 2014/15.

However, there was no self assessment tax to pay on their dividends for the previous 2013/14 tax year because Ann and Victor were basic-rate taxpayers (remember they reduced their dividends drastically while business conditions were tough).

Because the couple had no self assessment tax to pay for the previous tax year, they do not have to make any payments on account in respect of the current tax year.

Their one and only tax payment for 2014/15 is due on 31 January 2016.

On 31 January 2016 they will also have to make a payment on account for the next 2015/16 tax year. This will be followed by a second payment on 31 July 2016.

Each payment on account is half the previous year's £22,241 self-assessment tax:

- 31 January 2016   £11,120.50 (£5,560 each)
- 31 July 2016   £11,120.50 (£5,560 each)

If Ann and Victor's business continues to thrive and they continue to pay themselves large dividends they will have to keep making these early income tax payments.

Instead of postponing their tax bill by 666 days, they will pay half their tax bill after roughly 300 days and the other half after roughly 480 days. Although their tax deferral period is on average nine months shorter, they are still doing far better than someone who has all their income tax deducted at source.

How to Avoid Payments on Account

Where the self-assessment liability for the current year can reasonably be expected to be less than that for the previous year, a taxpayer may apply to reduce payments on account to the appropriate level (i.e. half of the anticipated liability for the current year).

Hence, if Ann and Victor decide not to take taxable dividends in the 2015/16 tax year, they can apply to reduce their payments on account due on 31 January and 31 July 2016 to zero. They can do this when they submit their 2014/15 tax returns.

They can then pay themselves another big dividend at the start of the 2016/17 tax year, on 6 April 2016. There will be no payments on account with respect to this income because they had no self assessment tax to pay for the previous 2015/16 tax year.

What this means is that by paying big taxable dividends every second year, Ann and Victor can completely avoid having to make payments on account.

They can still pay themselves a tax-free dividend, to use up their basic-rate bands in the intervening years because this creates no self assessment tax liability and hence no payments on account. For example:

2014/15	Big taxable dividend
2015/16	Small tax-free dividend
2016/17	Big taxable dividend
2017/18	Small tax-free dividend

And so on...

In this way, the full 666 days of tax deferral will be preserved on every payment!

Cashflow isn't everything, of course, and there may be other tax planning considerations. For example, if you expect to pay tax at a higher marginal rate in a future tax year, you may be better off taking more dividends in an earlier tax year.

Part 6

Splitting Income with Your Family

Chapter 20

Splitting Income with Your Spouse or Partner

In Chapter 9 it was shown that a couple may be able to double up the tax-free salary and dividend.

That's all very well if the couple own and run the company together. But what if your spouse/partner isn't involved in the business, for example if the company was started before you met or if your spouse/partner has a separate career and receives salary income from another employer?

In situations like these it may be possible to save income tax by gifting shares in the company to your spouse. It may even be possible to save more tax by paying them a salary as well.

How much tax can be saved depends on individual circumstances, for example how much profit the company makes and how much taxable income each person has already.

A few years ago there were essentially just two effective tax rates for dividend income: 0% for basic-rate taxpayers (or those with no income at all) and 25% for higher-rate taxpayers.

If the company owner was a higher-rate taxpayer and their spouse was a basic-rate taxpayer, tax could be saved by paying the low earner sufficient dividend income to use up their personal allowance and basic-rate band.

Nowadays, it is possible to pay income tax at more than 25% on dividend income that falls into any of the following tax brackets:

- £50,000-£60,000   At least 37%
- £100,000-£120,000   37.5% to 46%
- Over £150,000   30.6%

(Note: these are the tax rates applying to cash dividends although the thresholds apply to gross dividends.)

If your income falls into one of these tax brackets you may be able to save even more tax by transferring shares in the business to your spouse.

You may even be able to save income tax if your spouse is already a higher-rate taxpayer and would pay 25% tax on any dividends received from the company.

Before we look at some sample tax savings it is important to point out that there are also potential dangers when it comes to splitting income with your spouse in this fashion. We will return to this important issue later in the chapter.

Capital Gains Tax

If you wish to split your dividend income with your spouse you generally have to transfer shares in the company to them.

In the case of married couples, a transfer of shares would be exempt from capital gains tax.

In the case of unmarried couples it gets a bit more complicated. Any transfer of shares in the business would be treated as if a sale has taken place at market value. However, the couple may be able to jointly elect to claim holdover relief. What this means is that the transfer is treated as having taken place at a price equal to the original purchase price of the shares. This means there will be no capital gains tax payable on the transfer.

To qualify for holdover relief, however, the company must generally be a regular trading company.

Unmarried couples who want to split their income face a further potential danger (see below).

Giving the Business Away

To successfully split your dividend income with your spouse it is essential that proper ownership of shares in the company is handed over. This means your spouse must be able to do what they like with any dividends paid out and with any capital growth from any sale of the business.

As we shall see shortly, it is also safer to transfer ordinary shares rather than shares that have fewer voting rights or other rights.

It is probably advisable to have any dividends received by your spouse paid into a separate bank account in their name, to illustrate to HMRC that you have not retained control of the money.

Dividends are generally payable in proportion to shareholdings. So if you normally take a dividend of £100,000 and want to transfer £40,000 of this income to your spouse, you will generally have to transfer 40% of the business to them.

Because this sort of tax planning, if done correctly, involves effectively giving away ownership and control of part of your business, it is only suitable where there is a significant amount of trust between the parties involved.

How Much of the Business Should Be Transferred?

For many company owners, a 50:50 ownership split with their spouse or partner will prove optimal, but a smaller stake can be transferred if the founder wants to retain more control over the business.

Example

Steve owns 100% of Steve's Spices, a small trading company. Steve currently pays himself a salary of £15,000 and cash dividends of £75,000 per year (gross dividends of £83,333).

His total income is £98,333 which means he is close to the £100,000 threshold. If his income rises above this threshold he will start to lose his income tax personal allowance.

He currently pays income tax of £12,705 on his dividend income (£98,333 - £41,865 x 22.5% – see Chapter 3 for an explanation of how dividends are taxed).

Steve's wife Lara does not own any shares in the company but she does receive rental income of £8,000 from buy-to-let properties.

At present £33,865 of her income tax personal allowance and basic-rate band are being wasted (£41,865 - £8,000).

This means she can receive tax-free cash dividends of £30,479 tax free (£33,865 x 0.9).

Steve therefore transfers 40% of the ordinary shares in the business to Lara. The company continues to pay total dividends of £75,000 but now Steve's cash dividend is £45,000 and Lara's is £30,000.

Lara's total taxable income is £41,333, made up of gross dividend income of £33,333 and rental income of £8,000. Because her income is below the higher-rate threshold she does not pay any income tax on her dividend income.

Steve's total taxable income is now £65,000, made up of gross dividend income of £50,000 and salary income of £15,000. He now pays income tax of £5,205 on his dividends (£65,000 - £41,865 x 22.5%).

The tax on the total dividend income has been reduced by £7,500.

Furthermore, Steve's income is now well below the £100,000 threshold which means he doesn't have to worry about losing his income tax personal allowance for now.

If Steve transferred more of the business to Lara she would start paying 25% income tax on any additional cash dividends just like him (although she does have a tiny amount of her basic-rate band left over).

However, additional tax savings may be achieved if the couple are currently receiving child benefit. As we know from Chapter 12, the child benefit charge is payable if the highest earner in the household has income of more than £50,000. The maximum charge is payable once your income reaches £60,000.

As things stand, Steve will pay the maximum child benefit charge because his income is £65,000.

If, however, he transferred 50% of the business to Lara his total taxable income would fall to £56,667.

Lara will pay roughly the same amount of income tax on the additional dividends as Steve would have.

However, because Steve's income is now less than £60,000 the child benefit charge will be reduced (by approximately one third).

He could avoid the charge altogether by making a gross pension contribution of £6,667, taking his adjusted net income down to £50,000.

This could save Steve and Lara an additional £1,771 in 2014/15 if they have two children (see Chapter 12).

Spouse Has No Taxable Income

This is the 'bread and butter' scenario. The company owner is a higher-rate taxpayer; the spouse is a 'house-spouse' with no job and no other taxable income.

The spouse can receive gross dividends of up to £41,865 in 2014/15 (£37,679 cash dividends). The maximum potential tax saving is £9,420 if the other spouse is a higher-rate taxpayer (£37,679 x 25%).

If the company owner is an additional rate taxpayer (income over £150,000) the potential tax saving would be £11,530 (£37,679 x 30.6%).

Spouse is a Basic-Rate Taxpayer

Another potentially common scenario. The company owner is a higher-rate taxpayer; their spouse has some taxable income but is a basic-rate taxpayer (income under £41,865 in 2014/15). The spouse's taxable income could come from a job, a sole trader business, rental properties etc.

For example, let's say your spouse already has taxable income of £30,000 from other sources. They can receive tax-free gross dividends of up to £11,865 in 2014/15 (£10,679 in cash dividends). The potential tax saving is £2,670 (£10,679 x 25%).

If the company owner is an additional rate taxpayer the potential tax saving would be £3,268 (£10,679 x 30.6%).

Spouse is a Higher-Rate Taxpayer

In this situation both partners have taxable income of more than £41,865 (2014/15 figures). The spouse's income comes from other sources.

In this situation paying dividends to the spouse will only produce a tax saving if the company owner pays income tax at *more than 25%*, i.e. their income falls into one of the 'extortionate' tax bands listed at the beginning of the chapter.

For example, if the company owner is an additional rate taxpayer any dividends paid to their spouse will be taxed at 25% instead of 30.6%. Potential tax saving: £560 per £10,000 of cash dividends paid.

There are many reasons why any tax savings that may be achieved in one tax year by splitting income with your spouse may not be achievable in full in future tax years, including:

- Changes to tax rates and thresholds
- Changes to personal circumstances

Changes to Tax Rates & Thresholds

The additional rate applying to income over £150,000 was reduced on 6 April 2013. The effective tax rate applying to cash dividends was reduced from 36.1% to 30.6%. The potential tax saving that can be achieved by transferring dividend income to a spouse who is a higher-rate taxpayer has been reduced from £1,110 per £10,000 of cash dividends to £560.

Of course, where your spouse is a basic-rate taxpayer and can receive tax-free dividends the savings are still impressive: 30.6% tax versus 0% tax.

The Government has stated that it is committed to abolishing the additional rate altogether but this will be politically difficult and no firm date has been provided. If the rate were to be abolished this could eliminate the tax savings currently achieved from shifting dividend income to a spouse who is a *higher-rate* taxpayer.

Changes to Personal Circumstances

The income tax savings obtained by splitting income with a spouse are only achieved if the current company owner has a higher marginal income tax rate than their spouse.

It is possible that, over time, the original company owner's marginal income tax rate will fall and/or the tax rate of his spouse will increase. This could eliminate or even reverse any initial income tax saving that is achieved.

The original company owner's marginal tax rate could fall if the company's profits fall, resulting in lower dividends. The marginal tax rate of a spouse could rise if their income from other sources increases (for example, if a sole trader business they own produces bigger profits).

There are lots of different permutations. The key point is that couples should look further ahead than just one tax year when deciding what proportion of the company each should own.

HMRC's Attacks on Income Shifting

Income splitting arrangements like those described in this chapter have come under attack in recent years. In particular, the taxman has tried to prevent dividends being paid to non-working spouses or spouses who do just a small amount of work for the company.

In particular, the taxman's target has been small 'personal service' companies (IT consultants and the like) where most of the work is carried out by one person.

It all came to a head in the notorious 'Arctic Systems' tax case. HMRC tried to use the so-called settlements legislation to prevent Geoff Jones, a computer consultant, from splitting his dividend income with his wife.

The settlements legislation is designed to prevent income being shifted from one individual to another via a 'settlement', for example by transferring an asset or making some other 'arrangement'.

In the Arctic Systems case Mr Jones did most of the work in the company. Mrs Jones did a few hours admin each week. Because Mr Jones only paid himself a small salary despite all the work he did, more money was left to pay out as dividends to Mrs Jones. HMRC therefore decided that a settlement had taken place and tried to have Mrs Jones' dividend income taxed in her husband's hands.

HMRC originally won the case but the decision was overturned by the House of Lords.

The judges agreed with HMRC that a settlement had taken place **but** decided that the settlement provisions could not be applied because in this case the couple were protected by the exemption for gifts between spouses. This exemption applies where:

- There is an outright gift of property to a spouse, and
- The property is not wholly or mainly a right to income

On the first point, the judges ruled that, although Mrs Jones had subscribed for her share when the company was set up (i.e., it was not strictly speaking gifted to her by her husband), her share was essentially a gift because it contained an 'element of bounty': the share provided a benefit that Mr Jones would not have given to a complete stranger.

On the second point, the judges also ruled that a gift of *ordinary* shares is not wholly or mainly a right to income because ordinary shares have other rights: voting rights and the right to capital gains if the company is sold.

Thanks to the courage of Mr and Mrs Jones, who were prepared to fight HMRC all the way to the House of Lords, this exemption should safeguard most types of income splitting arrangements between married couples where ordinary shares are involved.

For this reason many tax advisers are of the opinion that married couples should make hay while the sun shines, i.e. they should split their dividend income with their spouses while they can.

Preference Shares

The outcome of the Arctic Systems case may have been different if another type of share other than ordinary shares had been involved.

In another tax case (*Young v Pearce*), wives were issued with preference shares that paid income but had very few other rights. The shares did not have voting rights and did not entitle the spouses to receive any payout in the event of the company being sold (other than the original £25 payment for the shares).

All that the preference shares provided was a right to receive 30% of the company's profits as a dividend. The court therefore decided that the preference shares provided wholly or mainly a right to income. Thus the exemption for gifts between spouses was not available and the settlement rules applied. The wives' dividends were therefore taxed in the hands of their husbands.

Unmarried Couples & Other Family Members

Although HMRC was defeated in the Arctic Systems case, the judges did agree that a settlement had taken place. The taxpayers only won the case thanks to the exemption for gifts between *spouses*.

There is now uncertainty as to where this leaves income-splitting arrangements between other groups of individuals, in particular, *unmarried* couples.

HMRC probably does take the view that the settlements legislation applies to unmarried couples and other family members, especially where small personal service companies are involved.

However, to date the taxman has not pursued these individuals aggressively so, again, it may be a case of making hay while the sun shines.

To protect against any potential attack the best defence is probably to have both individuals equally involved in the business (a bit of admin or bookkeeping will not suffice, as Mr and Mrs Jones discovered.)

HMRC's main concern seems to be personal service companies (IT consultants and other businesses where the profits are generated from one person's services). Larger businesses that have other employees, premises, equipment etc may be safer because the profits come from various sources, not just the work of one individual.

Danger Ahead?

In 2007 draft income shifting legislation was published but fortunately never made it onto the statute books after being widely condemned for being completely unworkable.

That draft legislation essentially sought to prevent business owners from receiving dividends unless they effectively earned them! This goes against the whole basis of shareholder capitalism – dividends are supposed to be a reward for being an entrepreneur and setting up or investing in a business.

Although income shifting legislation is on the back burner for now, it could be introduced in the future and could upset some income splitting arrangements.

If legislation is introduced eventually it may be important to demonstrate that the shareholders are fully involved in the business.

Salaries for Spouses

If your partner also works for your company they can be paid a salary. Please note, you cannot pay them a salary if they do no work for the company. And you cannot pay them more than the market rate. If you do, the company will be denied tax relief for the expense.

If your partner has no taxable income from other sources, a small salary will be more tax efficient than simply paying them dividends.

Why? Unlike dividends which are paid out of the company's after-tax profits, salaries are a tax deductible expense for the company.

In other words, in addition to any *income tax* savings enjoyed by couples who split their income, a salary will also save the company *corporation tax*.

For example, a small salary of £7,956 will save a small company £1,591 in corporation tax.

To avoid national insurance salary payments should be made monthly instead of as a lump sum. If, however, your spouse is a director the payment can be made as a lump sum because company directors pay national insurance on an annual basis.

Second Jobs

What if your spouse already has income from other sources, e.g. a salary from another job? Is it still tax efficient to get your company to pay them a salary?

Firstly, it's important to point out that, if your spouse works for another employer, the employment contract may prevent them working for you as well.

Even if there is no such restriction, it is usually not more tax efficient to receive a salary where there is income from other sources that uses up all of the individual's income tax personal allowance (although there may be other reasons why a salary is desirable – see Chapter 7 and Part 8).

Chapter 21

Splitting Income with Your Children

Tax-free Dividends

It is possible to gift shares in your company to your children. Because they will have their own income tax personal allowance and basic-rate band it may be possible for them to receive tax-free dividends of up to £37,679 each in 2014/15.

However, it is important to point out that this type of tax planning generally only works when *adult* children are involved (i.e. children 18 or older).

Transfers of income to minor children are generally ineffective and the income would be taxed in the parent's hands.

This section therefore deals exclusively with adult children.

If you gift shares in the company to your adult children there will potentially be capital gains tax payable, as if you had sold the shares to them for their full market value. However, it may be possible for both the parent and child to jointly elect to hold over the capital gain.

To qualify for holdover relief the company must, generally speaking, be a trading company.

The safest route is probably to use ordinary shares, which means your children will obtain full ownership and voting rights in respect of their share of the business, not just a right to receive dividends.

There is a potential tax trap for family members who are gifted shares and are also employees of the company.

In certain cases, where shares are obtained because of an individual's employment, a gift of shares can be subject to employment income tax charges.

However, there is an exemption where shares are given in the 'normal course of domestic, family or personal relationships'. So in most family companies, where shares are transferred to a spouse or adult children, the transfer should not give rise to any employment tax charges.

There is nevertheless a danger that, in certain circumstances, HMRC may argue that the individuals received shares by virtue of their employment, not because they are family members.

For example, if the individual only receives a small salary from the company (i.e. below market rate) HMRC may have more grounds to argue that the gift was made to increase the individual's remuneration from the company.

If shares are transferred to a family member who is an employee and to other employees who are not family members, this could indicate that the gift was made because of the family member's employment.

On the other hand, if shares are gifted to several family members (some of whom are not employees) this may indicate that the gift was made solely because of the family relationship.

It may be wise in such circumstances to document the reasons for the gift and (as always) obtain professional advice.

Salaries for Children

It's often worth getting your company to employ your children (including your minor children) at certain points in time. The salary payments will generally be a tax deductible expense for the business, providing the payments can be justified by the duties performed.

Furthermore, the income will generally be tax free in the hands of the children, if they're at school or university and have no other taxable income.

A tax deduction coupled with a tax-free receipt is the best possible outcome when it comes to extracting money from your company!

Those aged under 16 can be paid up to £10,000 in 2014/15 with no income tax or national insurance consequences.

When the child reaches 16 national insurance becomes payable. Your company will pay 13.8% employer's national insurance on any income over £7,956 (unless the company has spare employment allowance) and the child will pay 12% employee's national insurance.

Starting in 2015 employers will not have to pay national insurance on salaries paid to under 21s who are basic-rate taxpayers. The employees themselves will, however, have to pay national insurance.

It is important to take note of the restrictions placed on the hours and types of work that children can do because this will affect how much you can pay them.

Restrictions on Work and Hours

Children are of compulsory school age up to the last Friday in June in the academic year of their 16th birthday. After this they are at the 'mandatory school leaving age' and can apply for a national insurance number and work full time.

Until that time there are restrictions on the hours and types of work that can be carried out. For starters, it is generally illegal to employ children under 13 in any capacity (unless they're involved in TV and modelling).

Other children must not work:

- Without an employment permit if local byelaws require it
- In factories or on industrial sites
- During school hours
- Before 7.00 am or after 7.00 pm
- For more than 1 hour before school (local byelaws permitting)
- For more than 4 hours without taking a 1 hour break
- In occupations prohibited by byelaws/legislation (e.g. pubs)
- If the work will harm their health, well-being or education
- Without having a 2 week break during the school holidays in each calendar year

More Restrictions on Hours Worked

During term time children can work for no more than 12 hours per week including a maximum of:

- 2 hours on school days and Sundays
- 5 hours on Saturdays for 13 to 14 year olds; 8 hours for 15 to 16 year olds

During school holidays 13 to 14 year olds may work a maximum of 25 hours per week. This includes a maximum of:

- 5 hours on weekdays and Saturdays
- 2 hours on Sunday

During school holidays 15 to 16 year olds may work a maximum of 35 hours per week. This includes a maximum of:

- 8 hours on weekdays and Saturdays
- 2 hours on Sunday

National Minimum Wage

If your children are below the compulsory school leaving age the national minimum wage does not apply. From 1 October 2014 the hourly rates for older children will be as follows (current rates in brackets):

- £6.50 (£6.31)   main rate age 21 and over
- £5.13 (£5.03)   age 18 to 20
- £3.79 (£3.72)   age 16 to 17 if above school leaving age
- £2.73 (£2.68)   apprentice rate

Part 7

Other Profit Extraction Strategies

Chapter 22

Loans to Directors

It used to be illegal for companies to make loans to directors. This is no longer the case. Since October 2007, loans of any size have been permitted.

With the exception of loans for under £10,000 they do generally have to be approved by the company's shareholders.

Obviously, for most small companies, this is not a problem because the shareholders and directors are the same people!

You cannot take a loan from your company for an indefinite period without any tax consequences. If that were possible most company owners would never pay themselves taxable dividends.

The attractiveness of taking a loan from your company is limited by two potential tax charges:

- a 25% company tax charge (section 455 charge)
- a benefit-in-kind charge

Fortunately, it is possible to avoid or mitigate the damage caused by these taxes, if you understand the rules.

Before explaining how these tax charges operate it is worth pointing out that there's probably not much point taking a loan from your company if you are a basic-rate taxpayer (income under £41,865 in 2014/15).

Why? Because you can just pay yourself a tax-free dividend instead!

The Section 455 Charge

Most private companies are 'close companies'. If you are a director/shareholder of a close company you are known as a 'participator'. Some other shareholders are also classed as participators.

If a company lends money to a participator *the company* will have to pay a 25% tax charge on the loan. This is known as the section 455 charge (previously known as the section 419 charge). Failure to pay this charge will result in penalties and interest.

However, there are two reasons why this charge is not as bad as it first appears:

#1 Short-term Loans Escape the Section 455 Charge

The 25% tax does not apply if the loan is repaid within nine months of the company's financial year end. This is the normal due date for the company's corporation tax.

This means that short-term loans to directors do not attract a tax charge.

Example

Bill Ltd's financial year ends on 31 December 2014. The company makes a £10,000 loan to Bill, the sole shareholder and director, in January 2014.

Bill repays the loan before the end of September 2015. The company will not have to pay the 25% tax charge because the loan was repaid within 9 months of the end of the accounting period in which it was made.

Example

The facts are the same as before except only £7,000 is repaid before the end of September 2015. The remaining £3,000 is repaid in October 2016. The company will pay a section 455 tax charge of £750 (£3,000 x 25%).

140

#2 The Section 455 Charge is Refundable

Even if the 25% tax does end up being paid because the loan is not repaid early enough, the tax will be refunded when the loan is repaid.

That's the good news. The bad news is the company will only be repaid 9 months after the end of the accounting period in which the loan is repaid.

In Bill Ltd's case this means the £750 tax will be repaid on 1 October 2017.

Exemption for Minority Shareholders

This exemption isn't much use to most small company owners. Nevertheless it is worth mentioning that there is no 25% company tax charge if you own 5% or less of the company's ordinary shares.

There are a number of qualifying criteria:

- Total loans to the individual cannot exceed £15,000
- The individual must work full time in the business

When it comes to the 5% limit you must include shares owned by you, your spouse and other 'associates' (e.g. close relatives).

Although there is no company tax charge on small loans to minority shareholders, there will still be a potential benefit-in-kind charge.

Benefit-in-kind Charge

If no interest is payable on the loan or if the interest paid is less than the 'official rate', the director will have to pay an income tax benefit-in-kind charge.

The official rate is currently 3.25%, so if the interest charged on the loan is less than this, a benefit-in-kind charge is payable.

For example, if the loan is for £20,000 and no interest is charged, the director will face the following benefit-in-kind charge if he is a higher-rate taxpayer:

£20,000 loan x 3.25% interest x 40% tax = £260

The company will also have to pay class 1A national insurance:

£20,000 loan x 3.25% interest x 13.8% = £89.70

The benefit in kind is reduced if interest is paid to the company. For example, if you pay 1% interest, the benefit in kind will be calculated using an interest rate of 2.25% (3.25% less 1%).

Note, however, that the benefit in kind is only reduced if there is a formal obligation to pay interest to the company. For this reason it is probably advisable to have a properly drawn up loan agreement.

If you do pay interest on the loan, the good news is that you will be paying the money to your own company rather than a bank. However, the company will pay corporation tax on the interest it receives.

It must also be remembered that money inside a company is generally less valuable than money outside a company. If you wish to withdraw the interest back out as a dividend, there could be an income tax charge.

Should Directors Pay Interest?

Let's compare two scenarios:

- An interest-free loan
- Paying interest at the official rate

We will assume that the loan is for £20,000, the official interest rate is 3.25%, the director is a 40% taxpayer and the company pays 20% corporation tax.

#1 Interest-free loan

The benefit-in-kind charge paid by the director will be:

$$£20,000 \times 3.25\% \times 40\% = £260$$

The national insurance paid by the company will be:

$$£20,000 \times 3.25\% \times 13.8\% = £90$$

The employer's national insurance is itself a tax deductible expense, so for most small companies the net cost would actually be £72 (£90 less 20% corporation tax relief).

$$\text{Total cost of loan: } £260 + £72 = £332$$

#2 Interest at the official rate

On a £20,000 loan the director will pay £650 interest to the company (£20,000 x 3.25%). The company will then pay 20% corporation tax on this interest, so the total cost is £130:

$$£650 \times 20\% \text{ corporation tax} = £130$$

Even if the interest is taken back out as a dividend, producing an income tax charge of £163 for a higher-rate taxpayer (£650 x 25%), the total tax cost will be less than for an interest-free loan.

In summary, it is generally cheaper, at present, to pay interest at the official rate, rather than take an interest-free loan.

The Official Rate of Interest

The official rate of interest was recently reduced from 4% to 3.25%. Back in 2009 it was 6.25%. If and when interest rates are eventually increased, the official rate of interest will also be increased and this will affect the cost of directors' loans.

The current and previous official rates can be found here:

www.hmrc.gov.uk/rates/interest-beneficial.htm

Exemptions from the Benefit in Kind Charge

There are two important exemptions from benefit in kind charges:

- Loans to invest in another company
- Loans for less than £10,000 (£5,000 before 6 April 2014)

Note that neither of these two exemptions make any difference to the requirement to pay the section 455 company tax charge.

Remember, however, that the company tax charge does not apply to short-term loans (up to 21 months) and is repayable.

Benefit-in-kind exemption #1
Loans to invest in another company

There is generally no benefit in kind charge on *qualifying* loans. A qualifying loan is one where the interest (if interest was charged) would be tax deductible.

An example of a qualifying loan would be one given to an individual so that he can invest in another private trading company or property investment company.

The person borrowing the money must generally hold more than 5% of the ordinary shares in the company in which the money is being invested.

The business exemption could be useful if you have surplus cash sitting inside one company and want to invest it in a second company (either a regular trading business or a company that invests in rental properties). It allows you to borrow from one company to invest in another company without being subject to a benefit-in-kind charge.

Remember, however, that the section 455 company tax charge still applies, unless the loan is repaid within 9 months of the end of the accounting period in which it is made.

Benefit-in-kind exemption #2
Loans under £10,000

There is no benefit-in-kind charge if all of the loans to the director/shareholder total £10,000 or less throughout the tax year. This limit was raised from £5,000 to £10,000 on 6 April 2014.

It is important to understand that any sum due from the director to the company is counted as a 'loan', including goods or services that have been provided to the director but not paid for.

The section 455 corporation tax charge still applies if the loan is not repaid on time. Nevertheless, this exemption currently allows a director/shareholder to take a loan of up to £10,000 for up to 21 months with no adverse tax consequences.

Even if you just take the money and stick it in a cash ISA, the exemption may provide an opportunity to save some tax and earn more interest. Company accounts often pay much less interest than the best deals on individual savings accounts.

Example

Let's say Jack and Jill, both directors of Jack and Jill Ltd, take loans of £10,000 each (£20,000 in total) at the beginning of the company's financial year. They stick the money in ISAs earning 1.5% tax free.

They repay the loans 21 months later, just in time to prevent the company paying the 25% section 455 tax charge. In total, they will have earned around £500 tax free, compared with the £35 or so of taxable interest the company would have earned.

Larger Short-term Loans

In the above example, by taking a loan for no more than £10,000 and repaying it on time, both the 25% section 455 tax charge and the benefit-in-kind charge were avoided.

What if you want to borrow more than the tax-free limit for a short period – how does this compare with paying yourself additional taxable dividends?

Example

Penelope owns Pitstop Hotels Ltd. The company pays 20% corporation tax and has a 31 December accounting date. Penelope normally withdraws a small salary and enough dividend income to use up her basic-rate band (the tax-free amounts discussed in Chapters 6 and 8).

It's the beginning of January 2015 and Penelope would like to withdraw an additional £20,000 from Pitstop Hotels, over and above her usual tax-free salary and dividends. She intends to use the money to pay for some home improvements.

If she takes the money as a dividend there will be an income tax charge of £5,000 payable by 31 January 2016.

Instead she decides to takes a loan of £20,000 from her company on 1 January 2015. Because the loan is for more than £10,000 she will be subject to a benefit-in-kind charge, unless she pays interest to her company at the official rate.

The loan will also be subject to the 25% section 455 tax charge unless it is repaid by the end of September 2016 (9 months after the end of the company's accounting period on 31 December 2015).

She decides to pay interest to her company at the official rate and to repay the loan on 20 September 2016, i.e. after 629 days (she doesn't want to cut it too fine). Assuming there is no change to the official rate of interest, the total interest payable to Pitstop Hotels will be £1,120:

$$£20,000 \times 3.25\% \times 629/365 = £1,120$$

The corporation tax payable on the interest is £224 (£1,120 x 20%). This is effectively the cost of the loan.

To repay the loan Penelope withdraws additional dividend income, over and above her regular tax-free amount, of £20,000 on 6 April 2016. The income tax on this additional dividend is £5,000, payable by 31 January 2018.

By taking a loan in 2015 instead of a taxable dividend, Penelope has managed to defer paying income tax of £5,000 for two years. The total cost is £224 which comes to just over 2% per year.

Additional points to note:

- If Penelope's marginal income tax rate in 2016/17 is significantly higher than in 2014/15 then she may be better off paying herself a dividend in January 2015 instead of taking a loan. In particular she may have to watch out for the £50,000, £100,000 and £150,000 thresholds.

- If Penelope can repay the loan out of her tax-free company income (i.e. without having to withdraw an additional *taxable* dividend) she may be able to save £5,000 in income tax, not just defer paying it.

Loans to Directors – Other Issues

Loans to Family

You cannot necessarily avoid the section 455 tax charge and benefit-in-kind charge by making loans to family members. For example, both the section 455 charge and the benefit-in-kind charge apply to loans to spouses and children of the director/shareholder and other close relatives. The section 455 charge also applies to loans to business partners.

The charges do not apply to loans to friends and some more distant relatives BUT you will incur the taxman's wrath if the benefit of the loan passes back to you or a close relative.

Loan Repayments & Waivers

If the loan is formally waived or written off by the company, the amount should be treated as a deemed dividend for income tax purposes.

However, HMRC may argue that the amount waived should be treated as earnings and subject to both income tax and national insurance (especially if the loan waiver/write-off is not approved at a general meeting of the shareholders).

The safest course of action may be to ensure that any loan is always repaid, wherever possible, rather than written off.

Paperwork

Although it's simple in small companies to obtain shareholder approval for loans, it's important to get the paperwork right. There should be a proper loan agreement with written documentation outlining the nature of the loan, the company's liability and the amount and purpose of the loan. The shareholders must then grant their approval at a meeting or by written resolution, again with all the appropriate documentation.

Shareholder approval is not required for loans of up to £10,000, although it is good practice to continue to produce the same paperwork, where possible, as this may provide more certainty as to the tax treatment of the borrowed money.

Loan Recycling

HMRC didn't like it when loans to directors were repaid before the 25% tax was payable, with new loans taken out straight away (known as 'bed and breakfasting'). Thus a number of changes came into operation on 20 March 2013:

The 30 Day Rule

Relief from the section 455 tax is denied if:

- A shareholder makes repayments totalling £5,000 or more to the company and within 30 days

- New loans totalling £5,000 or more are made to the same person or their associates

For this rule to apply, the original loan and repayment can take place in the same or different accounting periods. The new loan must be in a subsequent accounting period to the original loan.

It's important to point out that the 30-day rule does not apply where the loan is repaid using amounts that give rise to an income tax charge, for example where a taxable dividend is declared to clear the director's loan account.

Example 1

During accounting period 1 there is a loan outstanding of £6,000. Two days before the end of the accounting period £6,000 is repaid. Three days into accounting period 2 a new £6,000 loan is taken. The repayment will be matched with the new loan, not the old loan. The loan from accounting period 1 is treated as still outstanding and will be subject to the 25% tax charge if not repaid.

Example 2

C Ltd is a close company in which Jim is a shareholder. C Ltd's accounting period ends on 31 March 2014. On 25 March 2014, Jim borrows £15,000 from C Ltd. If the loan is not repaid within nine months and a day of the end of the accounting period, C Ltd must pay a 25% section 455 tax charge (£3,750).

On 1 December 2014, a dividend of £9,000 is declared by C Ltd on which Jim is chargeable to income tax. On the same day, Jim repays the remaining £6,000. On 10 December 2014, Jim borrows £3,500 from the company. On 15 December 2014, Jim borrows a further £2,000 from the company.

The section 455 tax charge is calculated as follows:

- £9,000 was repaid by applying a chargeable dividend towards the loan. This is ignored when it comes to applying the 30 day rule. The remaining £6,000 that Jim repays exceeds the £5,000 minimum repayment under the 30-day rule.

- Nine days later and 14 days later respectively (i.e. within 30 days) Jim withdraws a further £5,500 (£3,500 + £2,000) which is also in excess of the £5,000 limit for new loans.

- The new loans (£5,500) are less than the repayments (£6,000). Relief from the 25% tax is denied on the lesser amount of £5,500. Thus £1,375 is payable on 1 January 2015 (nine months and a day after the accounting period ends). Only the real repayment of £500 is recognised.

The Arrangements Rule

This rule applies even if the new borrowing takes place after 30 days. Relief from the section 455 tax will be denied if:

- Prior to repaying the loan, the total amount owed by the shareholder to the company is £15,000 or more, and

- At the time of the repayment, arrangements had been made for new loans of £5,000 or more to replace the amounts repaid.

The relief denied is the lower of the amount repaid and the new loan.

'Arrangements' are not defined and HMRC will give the term a wide meaning.

Once again, the arrangements rule does not apply if the loan is repaid with a taxable dividend or bonus. In other words, if a loan account is credited with a taxable dividend this will be treated as a valid loan repayment.

Example

Brigitte owes her company Bard Ltd £25,000 which she borrowed on 1 June 2014 during the accounting period ending 30 June 2014.

After the end of the accounting period, Brigitte takes a 45-day loan from the bank for £25,000 and uses it to repay the loan to her company. 40 days after repaying her company, Brigitte takes a new loan of £30,000 from her company and uses it to repay the bank.

There is a significant risk that HMRC will argue that, at the time she repaid her company, Brigitte had made arrangements to withdraw a new amount from her company (to repay the bank loan), so the original loan will be treated as not repaid. As a result, the section 455 tax will become payable on the initial £25,000 loan, unless a further repayment is made.

Chapter 23

Company Pays
You Rent

Should you get your company to pay you rent?

Many company owners own their business premises *personally* and the company pays them rent.

Paying yourself rental income is often more tax efficient than paying yourself a higher salary. Like salaries, rental payments are a tax deductible expense for the business (providing the rent does not exceed the market rent). But, unlike salaries, there is no national insurance cost.

But is rental income more tax efficient than dividend income? Sometimes, but not always, as we shall discover shortly.

Of course, there are many reasons why you may wish to pay yourself rental income instead of withdrawing dividends from your company.

For starters, to pay dividends the company must have sufficient distributable profits. There is no such requirement when it comes to paying rent.

Secondly, with rental income it is relatively straightforward to pay yourself a fixed monthly amount throughout the year, for example by setting up a direct debit from your company bank account to your personal bank account. This could be helpful if you have to personally pay various costs associated with the property, especially mortgage interest.

With rental income there is no requirement to continually do all the paperwork that often accompanies dividend payments, for example holding directors' board meetings and shareholder meetings.

But will you save yourself income tax by paying rental income instead of dividends?

It all depends on your personal circumstances, for example how much taxable income you have and the amount of tax deductible mortgage interest you have.

Example

Warren is a company owner and a higher-rate taxpayer. He personally owns the property out of which the company operates but the company currently doesn't pay him any rent. He does not have any tax deductible mortgage interest to offset.

During the current 2014/15 tax year he has decided to pay himself a small-tax free salary of £7,956. He also has other taxable income of £2,044 which uses up the balance of his £10,000 income tax personal allowance.

The rest of his income takes the form of dividends from his company. Some of Warren's dividends are tax free, being covered by his income tax basic-rate band, but because he is a higher-rate taxpayer, a significant chunk of his dividend income is taxed at an effective rate of 25%.

Let's say he now decides to get the company to pay him rental income of £12,000 per year. What impact will this have on his net after-tax disposable income?

After paying income tax at 20% on the rental income he will be left with £9,600.

However, the rental income will use up £12,000 of his basic-rate band, which means up to £12,000 of his <u>gross</u> dividend income (£10,800 of his cash dividend income) could now be subject to higher-rate tax. This could increase his income tax bill by up to £2,700 (£10,800 x 25%).

Warren is therefore left with a net after-tax sum of £6,900 (£9,600 - £2,700).

If instead the company had not paid him any rental income, the company would have been left with an extra £9,600 to pay out as dividends (£12,000 less 20% corporation tax) and Warren would have been left with a net sum of £7,200, after paying income tax at 25%.

In total, by getting the company to pay him rent, Warren is worse off by £300 (£7,200 - £6,900).

It all boils down to the peculiar way in which dividends are taxed and means that, if the rental income your company pays you uses up some of your basic-rate band, and this increases the tax payable on some of your dividend income, you could end up out of pocket.

The amount by which you could be worse off is equivalent to 2.5% of your rental income.

Mortgage Interest

Many company owners who personally own their business premises will also have a mortgage on which they personally pay the interest. These interest payments can be offset against your rental income, effectively making some or all of it 'tax free'.

Most company owners will instinctively realise that it would be foolish not to receive rental income if they also have mortgage interest to pay (or other tax-deductible property expenses). Tax-free rental income has to be better than a taxable dividend!

Nevertheless, let's compare the two scenarios to find out exactly how much better off Warren could end up. This will also help us answer a more relevant question: Is it tax efficient to *increase* the rent your company pays you?

Example continued

The facts are the same except Warren also has tax deductible mortgage interest of £12,000. This completely offsets his rental income which means he can receive a £12,000 tax-free payment from the company.

If instead he decided not to make the company pay him any rental income, he would be left with an extra £9,600 to pay out as dividends (£12,000 less 20% corporation tax) and could end up with just £7,200 after paying income tax at 25%.

All in all, by paying himself enough rent to cover his mortgage interest, he could be £4,800 better off (£12,000 - £7,200).

The next thing to consider is whether it is tax efficient for Warren to get his company to pay him rent over and above his mortgage interest (and other tax deductible expenses related to the property). In other words, is it tax efficient to pay Warren enough money so that he is making a rental profit?

This is the situation in which Warren found himself in the first example but it's worth reinforcing the point.

Example continued

The true market rent for Warren's property is actually £6,000 higher, so he decides to increase the rent the company pays him from £12,000 to £18,000. He is now making a £6,000 rental profit and, after paying income tax at 20%, is left with an additional £4,800.

However, the additional rental income will use up £6,000 of his basic-rate band, which means £6,000 of his <u>gross</u> dividend income (£5,400 of his cash dividend income) could now be subject to higher-rate tax. This could increase his income tax bill by £1,350 (£5,400 x 25%).

In summary, Warren is left with an additional sum of £3,450 (£4,800 - £1,350).

If instead Warren had decided not to pay himself the additional rental income, the company would have been left with an extra £4,800 to pay out as dividends (£6,000 less 20% corporation tax) and Warren would have been left with £3,600 after paying income tax at 25%.

All in all, Warren is better off to the tune of £150 by not paying the additional rental income (the saving is equivalent to 2.5% of his taxable rental profits).

What these examples illustrate is that it is tax efficient to get your company to pay you enough rental income to cover your mortgage interest and other tax deductible property costs.

However, it is not necessarily tax efficient to pay yourself any more rental income if this produces a taxable profit that uses up some of your basic-rate band, thereby increasing the tax payable on some of your dividend income.

Entrepreneurs Relief

Apart from saving income tax, there is an additional reason why it may be a good idea to get your company to pay you a rent that is lower than the true rental value of your trading premises: to save capital gains tax.

If you sell your business, you may be able to claim Entrepreneurs Relief which means you will pay 10% tax instead of up to 28% (see Chapter 25).

Trading premises can also qualify for Entrepreneurs Relief, even if you own them personally. However, you cannot claim Entrepreneurs Relief if your company has paid you a full market rent (although rent paid for periods before 6 April 2008 is ignored).

If your company pays you a rent that is lower than the market rent, or if you owned the property before 6 April 2008, then a partial claim for Entrepreneurs Relief can usually be made.

Chapter 24

Pensions: a Powerful Profit Extraction Device

Company directors, just like regular employees, can personally contribute up to 100% of their 'relevant UK earnings' to a pension. Your relevant UK earnings will typically include your:

- Salary and any bonus
- Taxable benefits in kind

Dividends do NOT count as earnings.

Basic-Rate Tax Relief

When you make pension contributions *personally* (as opposed to getting your company to make them) the taxman will top up your savings by paying cash directly into your pension. Effectively for every £80 you invest, the taxman will put in an extra £20.

Why £20? Your contributions are treated as having been paid out of income that has already been taxed at the basic income tax rate of 20%.

The company that manages your pension plan – usually an insurance company or SIPP provider – will claim this money for you from the taxman and credit it to your account.

So whatever contribution you make personally, divide it by 0.80 and you'll get the total amount that is invested in your pension pot. This is known as your gross pension contribution.

Example

Peter invests £4,000 in a self-invested personal pension (SIPP). After the taxman makes his top-up payment, the total amount of money Peter will have sitting in his pension pot is £5,000:

$$£4,000/0.80 = £5,000$$

Basic-rate tax relief isn't the end of the story. If Peter is a higher-rate taxpayer or additional rate taxpayer, he'll be able to claim even more tax relief, as we shall see shortly.

Company Pension Contributions

As a company owner you can also get your company (your employer) to make pension contributions on your behalf. Company pension contributions are always paid *gross* (there is no top up from the taxman) but the company will normally enjoy corporation tax relief on the payment.

For example, a small company making a pension contribution of £10,000 can claim corporation tax relief of £2,000 (£10,000 x 20% corporation tax relief).

Pension contributions made by employers are not restricted by the level of the employee's earnings. A company pension contribution can be bigger than the director's earnings. However, there are other restrictions on company pension contributions:

- Firstly, total pension contributions by you and your company must not exceed the £40,000 'annual allowance', although you can carry forward any unused allowance from the previous three tax years.

- Secondly, the company may be denied corporation tax relief on any pension contributions made on behalf of directors, if the taxman views them as 'excessive'. We'll return to this point later.

Company Directors with Small Salaries

As stated already, the pension contributions you make personally must not exceed your 'relevant UK earnings'. Salaries count as earnings; dividends do not.

For a company director taking the 'optimal' tax-free salary of £7,956, the maximum pension contribution that can be made is £7,956.

This is the maximum *gross* contribution. The director would personally invest £6,365 (£7,956 x 80%) and the taxman will top this up with £1,591 in basic-rate tax relief for a total gross contribution of £7,956.

For a company director taking a salary of £10,000 (for example, if there is spare employment allowance – see Chapter 6), the maximum gross pension contribution is £10,000. The director would personally invest £8,000 (£10,000 x 80%) and the taxman will top this up with £2,000 in basic-rate tax relief for a total gross contribution of £10,000.

Directors who want to make bigger pension contributions have two choices:

- Pay a bigger salary (i.e. more earnings)
- Get the company to make the contributions

In all situations, whether you want to make big pension contributions or small pension contributions, the key question is: "Who should make the pension contributions: me or the company?"

Answering this question is the main focus of this chapter.

Pension Contributions – You or the Company?

The short answer is this: If you want to make a relatively small pension contribution (no more than your small company salary) you should consider making the contribution *personally*. Additional contributions should be made by your company.

Why? Company directors who make contributions personally can generally enjoy up to 42.5% tax relief. Company pension contributions, on the other hand, effectively provide 40% tax relief if you are a higher-rate taxpayer – still very attractive but not quite as attractive.

Company directors enjoy this extra tax relief on the contributions they make personally thanks to an anomaly in the way gross dividends and gross pension contributions are calculated.

Let's now examine the issues with the help of some case studies.

Case Study 1
Company Director Makes Pension Contribution

Eva owns a small company called Cassidy Ltd. She takes a tax-free salary of £7,956 and a tax-free cash dividend of £30,518 for a total tax-free income of £38,474. She does not have any other taxable income.

If she makes a pension contribution with this level of income she will not be maximising her tax relief. She will not enjoy any higher-rate tax relief because she is a basic-rate taxpayer.

What she can do, if there are additional after-tax profits sitting in the company's bank account, is pay herself a bigger dividend. This would normally take Eva over the higher-rate threshold and be taxed but, coupled with a pension contribution, will be completely tax free.

Maximum Pension Contribution

Any pension contribution Eva makes personally cannot exceed her 'relevant UK earnings'. With a salary of £7,956, the maximum *gross* pension contribution she can make is £7,956.

This means Eva can personally invest £6,365 (£7,956 x 80%) and the taxman will add £1,591 in basic-rate tax relief for a total gross contribution of £7,956.

Optimal Additional Dividend

Eva extracts an extra cash dividend of £7,160. Note this is slightly more than the £6,365 she can personally invest in her pension. I'll explain why shortly. In the absence of a pension contribution, this dividend would be fully taxed because she has already utilised her income tax personal allowance and basic-rate band for the current tax year.

A cash dividend of £7,160 equates to a gross dividend of £7,956 (£7,160/0.9). As a higher-rate taxpayer now, Eva would normally pay 22.5% income tax on the additional dividend income, resulting in an income tax bill of £1,790.

Additional Dividend and Pension Contribution

Eva personally invests £6,365 of the additional £7,160 cash dividend in her pension. The taxman will add £1,591 in basic-rate tax relief for a total gross pension contribution of £7,956.

What about Eva's higher-rate tax relief? As per normal, her basic-rate band will be increased by the amount of her gross pension contribution.

Eva's gross pension contribution was £7,956, so her basic-rate band will be increased by £7,956 and all of her additional £7,956 gross dividend will be tax free instead of taxed at 22.5%.

Eva's higher-rate tax relief is:

$$£7,956 \times 22.5\% = £1,790$$

The tax on her additional dividend income has been eliminated.

In total, Eva will enjoy £3,381 of tax relief (£1,591 basic-rate relief plus £1,790 higher-rate tax relief). This comes to 42.5% of her £7,956 gross pension contribution.

Most higher-rate taxpayers only enjoy 40% tax relief on their pension contributions, so this is an attractive outcome.

Why 42.5% Tax Relief?

This 'bonus' 2.5% tax relief comes about thanks to an anomaly in the way higher-rate tax relief is given to those with dividend income.

Eva's cash pension contribution of £6,365 results in a gross pension contribution of £7,956 (£6,365/0.8). This allows her to claim higher-rate tax relief on all of her £7,956 additional gross dividend.

But she has only had to contribute £7,072 of gross dividends into her pension (£6,365/0.9) to produce a £7,956 gross pension contribution.

Thus she is enjoying higher-rate tax relief on an additional £884 of gross dividends, which saves her an extra £199 in tax:

$$£884 \times 22.5\% = £199$$

The extra £199 tax saving is 2.5% of her gross pension contribution:

$$£199/£7,956 = 2.5\%$$

Other pension savers do not enjoy this bonus tax relief. You normally only enjoy higher-rate tax relief on the income you actually invest in your pension.

Do All Company Directors Enjoy 42.5% Tax Relief?

Eva gets higher-rate tax relief on the entire additional £7,956 gross dividend she took out of her company.

If she had only taken an additional £7,072 of gross dividends – just enough to make the maximum pension contribution – her higher-rate tax relief would be:

$$£7,072 \times 22.5\% = £1,591$$

(Remember higher-rate tax relief is always restricted to the amount of income you have subject to higher-rate tax.)

Combined with her £1,591 in basic-rate tax relief, Eva would now enjoy only 40% tax relief, just like other taxpayers

$$£3,182/£7,956 = 40\%$$

The bottom line: As a company owner making pension contributions, you can enjoy 42.5% tax relief if you are a higher-rate taxpayer. Your gross dividends over the higher-rate threshold (£41,865 for 2014/15) must be at least as big as your gross pension contribution.

Final outcome: After making the pension contribution Eva has £7,956 in her pension pot and £39,269 of income, net of all taxes:

Original tax-free amounts	£38,474
Additional tax-free dividend	£7,160
Less: Cash pension contribution	£6,365
Total	£39,269

Case Study 2
Company Makes Pension Contribution

How would Eva fare if, instead of making the pension contribution personally, her company makes it?

The size of company contributions is not restricted by the level of an employee's earnings. However, for comparison purposes, we will assume that Cassidy Ltd also makes a £7,956 pension contribution (remember company pension contributions are always paid gross).

Eva will not obtain any tax relief personally but Cassidy Ltd will claim the amount as a corporation tax deduction. We will assume that Cassidy Ltd makes the contribution before the end of its accounting period, in other words before the company is subject to corporation tax on its profits.

To understand how a company pension contribution would affect Eva's financial position, we take the £7,160 of after-tax profits that she extracted as an additional dividend and add back the 20% corporation tax the company has to pay in the absence of a pension contribution:

Profits (£7,160/0.8)	£8,950
Less: Pension contribution	£7,956
Taxable profits	£994
Corporation tax @ 20%	£199
After-tax profits/cash dividend	£795
Income tax @ 25%	£199
After-tax dividend	£596

Eva's total after-tax income now consists of her initial tax-free dividend and salary and her additional after-tax dividend:

$$£38,474 + £596 = £39,070$$

As before, Eva has £7,956 sitting in her pension pot but her after-tax disposable income has fallen by £199 from £39,269 to £39,070.

Remember £199? That's the 2.5% bonus tax relief Eva enjoys when she makes the pension contribution personally.

In summary, Eva is better off making the pension contribution personally. Company pension contributions effectively produce 40% tax relief compared with 42.5% when the director makes them personally.

40% Tax Relief – Company Pension Contribution

Tax relief at 40% may be less than 42.5% but is not to be sneered at, especially by company directors like Eva who have low salaries and can therefore only make limited pension contributions personally.

Company pension contributions are an excellent way to extract additional money from your company in a tax-efficient manner.

But why do we say that company pension contributions produce 40% tax relief? In the above example Cassidy Ltd was only enjoying 20% corporation tax relief on the pension contribution it made for Eva. When it comes to company owners you have to look at the complete picture: the cost to both the director and the company of getting additional money out of the company.

If, instead of getting her company to make a tax-deductible pension contribution of £7,956, Eva had taken the income as a dividend, she and her company would pay the following taxes:

Pre-tax profits	£7,956
Corporation tax @ 20%	£1,591
After-tax profits/cash dividend	£6,365
Income tax @ 25%	£1,591
After-tax dividend	£4,774

The total extra tax would be £3,182 which is 40% of £7,956.

In summary, getting your company to make pension contributions could be a tax-efficient way to extract profits for your personal benefit. Total tax relief comes to 40%.

Additional Pension Contributions

Eva is better off making her pension contributions personally if she is happy to restrict them to the amount of her £7,956 tax-free salary.

If Eva wants to make an additional pension contribution in excess of her salary, she has two choices:

- Pay herself more salary (more earnings) and make the contribution personally

- Get the company to make the additional contribution

Paying more salary could be a bad idea from a tax-saving perspective because the additional salary will attract 12% employee's national insurance and 13.8% employer's national insurance (unless there is spare employment allowance).

Pension contributions made by individuals attract income tax relief but not national insurance relief.

Case Study 3
Additional Salary vs Company Contribution

Let's assume Eva wants to make an additional pension contribution of £10,000.

We'll assume she has taken the salary and dividends mentioned above and has made a pension contribution of £7,956 personally.

We'll also assume the company has pre-tax profits of £100,000. She now has two choices: pay an extra £10,000 of salary or get her company to make a £10,000 pension contribution.

Company's Position

	Company Makes Pension Contribution	Director Takes Additional Salary
	£	£
Pre-tax profits	100,000	100,000
Less:		
Salary	7,956	17,956
Employer's NI (13.8% over £7,956)	0	1,380
Company pension contribution	10,000	0
Net profits	82,044	80,664
Corporation tax @ 20%	16,409	16,133
After-tax profits	65,635	64,531
Less cash dividends:		
Initial dividend*	30,518	30,518
Additional dividend**	7,160	7,160
Remaining after-tax profits	**27,957**	**26,853**

* Initial tax-free divided to utilise the basic-rate band
** Additional dividend to fund director's own pension contribution

By getting the company to make the £10,000 pension contribution, instead of taking £10,000 of additional salary, the company is left with £1,104 more in its bank account.

This difference is down to the fact that employer's national insurance has to be paid on the additional salary but not on the company pension contribution.

The additional national insurance is £1,380 but this cost is a tax-deductible cost for the company so the net cost is £1,104 (£1,380 less 20% corporation tax relief).

Eva's personal position is examined below. The left-hand column shows how Eva fares when the company makes the £10,000 additional pension contribution.

This column contains all the numbers discussed in previous sections. Eva's after-tax income is completely unaffected by the company pension contribution.

The only difference is at the very bottom where her pension pot now has an extra £10,000 sitting in it.

The right-hand column shows how Eva fares with an additional £10,000 of salary and making the pension contribution personally.

She ends up £791 better off with a company pension contribution.

This difference is mainly down to the fact that she would have to pay £1,200 national insurance on the extra salary.

She has to pay £1,591 income tax but this is more than offset by £2,000 of basic-rate tax relief on the additional pension contribution. (£2,044 of the extra salary is tax free because she still has some of her income tax personal allowance remaining.)

In total, Eva and her company are better off to the tune of almost £2,000 by getting the company to make the additional pension contribution.

The savings can be explained by the additional national insurance cost of paying salaries.

In summary, the most tax-efficient strategy for many company directors is to make a relatively small pension contribution personally (no more than the tax-free company salary).

Thereafter, company pension contributions may be an excellent way to extract additional money from the company in a tax-efficient manner.

They are normally a tax-deductible expense and there is no income tax or national insurance payable on the amount.

Director's Position

	Company Makes Pension Contribution £	Director Takes Additional Salary £
Salary	7,956	17,956
Less:		
Employee's NI (salary - £7,956 x 12%)	0	1,200
Income tax (salary - £10,000 x 20%)	0	1,591
After-tax salary	**7,956**	**15,165**
Dividend Income		
Initial dividend	30,518	30,518
Additional dividend	7,160	7,160
Total cash dividends	37,678	37,678
Gross dividends (cash dividends/0.9)	41,865	41,865
Tax-free within basic-rate band:		
(£41,865 – salary)	33,909	23,909
Taxable gross dividend	7,956	17,956
Income tax @ 22.5%	1,790	4,040
Higher-rate tax relief:		
Gross pension contribution x 22.5%	1,790	4,040
After-tax cash dividends	**37,678**	**37,678**
Cash Pension Contributions		
Gross pension contributions x 0.8	6,365	14,365
Net Income	**39,269**	**38,478**
Pension Pot		
Cash pension contributions	6,365	14,365
Basic-rate relief	1,591	3,591
Company pension contributions	10,000	0
Total	17,956	17,956

Companies with Spare Employment Allowance

In Chapter 6 we showed why a salary of £10,000 is optimal when the company has spare national insurance employment allowance (even though £245 of employee's national insurance is payable).

With a salary of £10,000 the company owner can make a £10,000 gross pension contribution, with £8,000 coming from the director personally and £2,000 of tax relief from the taxman.

A company owner with a salary of £10,000 can also withdraw a tax-free dividend of £28,679. But he will not enjoy 42.5% tax relief on his pension contributions unless he has additional dividend income and is a higher-rate taxpayer (like Eva in Case Study 1).

For example, a company owner who wants to obtain 42.5% tax relief on a pension contribution of £10,000 needs to have additional gross dividend income of at least £10,000 (additional cash dividends of at least £9,000).

The company owner will be better off making the pension contributions personally if he is happy to restrict them to his £10,000 salary (because he will obtain 42.5% tax relief compared with 40% if his company makes the contributions).

If the company owner wants to make additional pension contributions he can either pay himself a higher salary and make the contributions personally or get the company to make them.

When there is spare employment allowance it makes no difference to the *company's* tax position whether it pays additional salary or makes the director's pension contributions (in contrast, Cassidy Ltd ends up £1,104 worse off by paying additional salary to Eva).

However, it does make a difference to the *company owner's* tax position. For example, an additional £10,000 of salary to fund a £10,000 pension contribution will leave the company owner worse off by £1,200 overall. This is because the additional salary attracts 12% employee's national insurance.

In summary, even if there is spare employment allowance, it is probably better to get the company to make any additional pension contributions rather than taking additional salary and making the contributions personally.

Restrictions on Company Pension Contributions

The important thing to note about company pension contributions is you do not need a dedicated company pension scheme to make them.

Most providers of personal pensions, like SIPPs, have special forms that allow your company to pay directly into them.

How much can the company contribute? The company's contributions are not limited to your salary earnings, but it is important to remember the annual allowance: the maximum total gross pension contributions that can be made by both you and your company may be limited to £40,000.

Furthermore, there is a danger that HM Revenue & Customs will deny corporation tax relief for 'excessive' pension contributions. Company pension contributions will only be a tax deductible expense if they are incurred wholly and exclusively for the purposes of the trade.

When determining whether company pension contributions qualify for corporation tax relief, HMRC will look at the total remuneration package of the director/shareholder. The total package (including salary, pension contributions and other benefits in kind) must not be excessive relative to the work the individual carries out and his or her responsibilities.

Relevant factors may include:

- The number of hours you work, your experience and your level of responsibility in the company.

- The pay of other similar employees in your company and other companies.

- The pay required to recruit someone to take over your duties.

- The company's financial performance.

Extra care may be necessary in the event of a large one-off company pension contribution.

It may be sensible to document the commercial justification (e.g. strong recent financial performance of the company) in the minutes of a directors' board meeting and hold a shareholders' meeting to approve the contribution.

Although the risk that your company will be denied corporation tax relief may be small, it is important to stress that, when it comes to company pension contributions, unlike many contributions made by individuals, there is no cast-iron guarantee that the company will enjoy tax relief.

That's why I would recommend speaking to a tax advisor before your company starts making significant contributions.

Chapter 25

Sell Your Business and Pay 10% Tax!

One of the most tax-efficient ways to grow your wealth is to build and then sell several companies during your working life.

This allows you to convert streams of heavily taxed income into low-taxed capital gains.

Many company owners who receive dividends have a marginal income tax rate of 25%. Those with income over £150,000 have a marginal tax rate of 30.6%.

But, when you sell a company and receive a cash lump sum, which replaces all of this heavily taxed income, you could end up paying just 10% tax, thanks to Entrepreneurs Relief.

At present you can have up to £10 million of capital gains taxed at 10% over your lifetime. This amount is doubled up in the case of couples.

Although serial entrepreneurs may pay much less tax than other business owners, this lifestyle is not for everyone. However, even if you only own one company it's still a good idea to have a basic understanding of the Entrepreneurs Relief rules in case you do eventually decide to cash in your chips.

With Entrepreneurs Relief there are certain things you need to check and do *before* you sell your company. Because this generous relief can save a couple up to £3,600,000 in capital gains tax, it's certainly worth knowing what you have to do to protect it!

If you are denied Entrepreneurs Relief you will pay capital gains tax at 28% if you are a higher-rate taxpayer.

Entrepreneurs Relief is available not just when you sell your company to a third party but can also be claimed if you wind up your company and extract the cash as a capital distribution (for example, following an asset sale by the company).

Qualifying for Entrepreneurs Relief

Company owners are entitled to Entrepreneurs Relief when they sell shares in the company. The main qualifying criteria are the following:

- The company must be your 'personal company', i.e. you must own at least 5% of the ordinary share capital and voting rights

- You must be an officer or employee of the company

- The company must be a 'trading' company

All three of these requirements must be met for at least one year before the business is sold. It does not matter if the requirements are met in earlier years.

The one-year rule means that you should be wary of incorporating any business within one year of selling it. To qualify for Entrepreneurs Relief you have to own the shares of the newly formed company for at least one year.

You should also be wary of transferring shares in the company to your spouse if a sale is anticipated. Transfers to spouses are exempt from CGT and your spouse can claim Entrepreneurs Relief when the business is sold, providing he or she satisfies the necessary conditions outlined above. The transfer would therefore usually have to be done at least one year before any sale is agreed.

Transfers to spouses were a useful way of increasing Entrepreneur Relief claims when the lifetime limit was just £1 million. Now that the limit has been raised to £10 million per person most company owners will not need to transfer shares to their spouses to reduce capital gains tax.

However, many company owners transfer shares to their spouses to reduce the income tax payable on dividends (see Chapter 20). If such a transfer were to take place within one year of selling the company, the recipient spouse will not be able to claim Entrepreneurs Relief.

Turning to the three qualifying criteria listed above, most small company owners will have no problem meeting the first two requirements. Company officers include non-executive directors and company secretaries, so you don't even have to work full-time at the company to qualify.

The third requirement could cause headaches for some company owners. Revenue and Customs regards the following as non-trading activities:

- Holding investment property
- Holding shares or securities
- Holding surplus cash

If there is substantial non-trading activity you could be denied Entrepreneurs Relief. Unfortunately to the taxman 'substantial' means as little as 20% of the company's:

- Assets
- Turnover
- Expenses
- Profits
- Directors' and employees' time

So, for example, if just 20% of the assets or income of the business are not trading assets or income, you may be denied Entrepreneurs Relief when you sell your business. As a result you may end up paying capital gains tax at 28% instead of 10%.

If your company doesn't own investment property or invest in other companies, the most serious danger is holding too much cash. If the taxman believes the cash is held for non-trading reasons (e.g. to avoid declaring taxable dividends), trading status could be revoked and Entrepreneurs Relief will be taken away.

However, this will not be a problem if you can prove that the cash was required for business purposes, for example as part of a well-documented expansion plan.

Some tax advisors argue that having a large cash balance may not pose a threat to an Entrepreneurs Relief claim if the cash was generated from trading activities and is not 'actively managed' like an investment.

However, it's all a bit of a grey area and professional advice is recommended. If the company does have surplus cash it may be necessary to extract it at least one year in advance to prevent the company's trading status being challenged.

In such cases you have to weigh up the potential costs and benefits: the benefit being a CGT rate of 10% instead of 28% and the cost being the income tax on any additional dividends.

Selling Property

Many business owners purchase business premises *personally* and rent them back to their company. The good news is Entrepreneurs Relief is available when "associated" assets like these are sold as part of an overall sale of the business. The bad news is that many business owners will not qualify for the maximum tax relief.

If the company pays you rent in respect of any period after 5 April 2008, your Entrepreneurs Relief will be restricted. The taxman's reasoning is that if the property is only available if rent is paid, it is an investment asset and not a business asset.

There are two pieces of good news here, however. Firstly, any rent receivable before April 2008 is disregarded and, secondly, rent paid at less than the market rate only leads to a partial reduction in the available Entrepreneurs Relief.

When Entrepreneurs Relief Does Not Save Tax

Where Entrepreneurs Relief is available it is generally more tax efficient for higher-rate taxpayers to retain profits inside the company (although not necessarily practical if you require funds personally).

However, claiming Entrepreneurs Relief is not always the most tax-efficient route when it comes to winding up/dissolving a company.

In some cases it is better to extract the company's cash as dividend income before the company is wound up.

If these dividends fall within the individual's basic-rate band they will be completely tax free. Adopting this strategy over several tax years could allow a significant amount of cash to be extracted from the company, especially when the tax-free amounts can be doubled up in the case of a company owned by a couple.

Similarly, when Entrepreneurs Relief is not available and capital gains tax is payable at 28%, taking dividends is often a better solution, unless your dividends are taxed at one of the 'extortionate' rates listed in Chapter 15.

Part 8

Salary & Dividends: Practical Issues & Dangers

Chapter 26

How to Avoid the National Minimum Wage

If you take a small salary from your company (for example, £7,956 or £10,000) there is a danger of falling foul of the national minimum wage regulations.

Where wages are too low, HMRC will force the company to make up the shortfall. Bigger wage payments may result in bigger national insurance bills for both the company and the director.

There is also a penalty equivalent to 100% of the unpaid wages with a maximum penalty of £20,000.

However, the key point to note about the national minimum wage is that it only applies to directors who have a contract of employment.

Due to the informal set up in many small companies, there may be some uncertainty as to whether an employment contract exists between the director and the company (employment contracts do not need to be in writing).

However, it is generally accepted amongst the tax profession that if you do not issue yourself with an explicit contract of employment the national minimum wage regulations will not apply.

This means you should be able to continue paying yourself a small salary, even if it is less than the national minimum wage.

However, risk averse company owners (those worried about potential penalties) should consider paying themselves enough salary to satisfy the national minimum wage regulations.

Directors with Contracts of Employment

If you do have a contract of employment the important point to note is that the national minimum wage does not apply to hours spent carrying out your duties as a director (or as a company secretary).

Of course, if you are involved full time in the management of your company the national minimum wage regulations will apply and you may need to pay yourself a bigger salary.

National Minimum Wage Rates

There are different levels of national minimum wage depending on your age. The main rate for those aged 21 and over is currently £6.31 per hour and will rise to £6.50 on 1 October 2014.

If you pay yourself a salary of £7,956 or £10,000 during 2014/15 this equates to around 24 to 30 hours per week of time spent actively managing the business.

If you spend, say, 35 hours per week actively managing your business, the total salary due for 2014/15 will be approximately £11,666:

$$35 \times 52 \text{ weeks} \times £6.41^* = £11,666$$

* Roughly the average minimum wage over the year

Fortunately this is not hugely higher than the optimal salary amounts but will still result in unwelcome national insurance charges.

The national insurance payable on this salary by the director would be £445 and £512 would be payable by the company (£0 if the company has spare employment allowance).

Of course, every case is different and some directors will be able to argue that they spend fewer hours actively managing the business.

Although it may seem that the best strategy is to simply not have a contract of employment, there may be others reasons why having such a contract is important.

Company Owners Who Aren't Directors

It is possible that some family members will be employees of the company but not directors. These individuals are subject to the national minimum wage for all hours spent working in the business (remember directors are exempt with respect to hours spent performing their duties as directors).

However, it is possible that if they only work part time, the salary that must be paid to them will still be within the optimal amounts of £7,956 or £10,000.

Chapter 27

Is My Salary Tax Deductible?

One of the benefits of getting your company to pay you a salary is that the amount will normally be a tax deductible expense and reduce the company's corporation tax bill.

However, it is important to point out that there is no automatic right to corporation tax relief. The amount paid has to be justified by the work carried out for the business and the individual's level of responsibility.

While this may not be an important issue for company owners who work full time in the business and pay themselves a small salary, it may be important if you start paying salaries to other family members, in particular those who only work on a part time basis.

The question of whether your employment income will attract corporation tax relief may also become an issue if you decide to pay yourself a large one-off bonus.

Some of the factors that may determine whether a salary or bonus payment is tax deductible include:

- The number of hours worked in the business

- The individual's legal obligations and responsibilities (e.g. directors' duties)

- The amount of pay received by the company's other employees

- The pay received by employees at other companies performing similar roles

- The company's performance and ability to pay salaries/bonuses.

In the case of large one-off bonus payments made only to the company's director/shareholders it may be necessary to document the commercial rationale for the payment to show that the payment is justifiable. This can be done in the minutes of a directors' board meeting.

It may also be advisable to record the approval of any bonus in the minutes of a shareholders' meeting.

Chapter 28

Salary vs Dividends: Non-Tax Factors

Most of this guide focuses on choosing the most tax efficient *level* of income and the most tax efficient *mix* of income (i.e. salary versus dividends).

However, when it comes to withdrawing money from your company there are lots of other non-tax factors that may need to be considered.

This chapter provides a short overview of some of the issues but is not definitive.

Cashflow and Working Capital Needs

When deciding how much income you withdraw from your company you must consider the cashflow and working capital requirements of the business.

It would naturally be irresponsible to pay yourself a large bonus or dividend if this affects the company's ability to carry on its business.

In some cases dividends can be declared even if left unpaid. This strategy could prove useful if the director/shareholder doesn't want to waste the annual 'tax-free dividend allowance' but also wants to help the company's cashflow.

If the director/shareholder is a higher-rate taxpayer income tax will still be payable on any dividends declared but not paid.

Dividends & Company Insolvency

Dividends should not be declared when the company is insolvent or if the payment of those dividends will render the company insolvent.

Dividends that are deemed illegal may have to be repaid, even if this results in the director being made bankrupt or being forced into an individual voluntary arrangement (IVA).

Company's Profitability

The payment of a large salary or bonus will depress the company's profits. This may affect the company's ability to borrow.

Directors Ability to Borrow

If you take a small salary and the rest of your income as dividends there is a possibility that this will affect your ability to borrow money personally.

Some lenders may only be interested in the level of your salary and ignore your dividends, being unfamiliar with this sort of pay structuring.

Other lenders, on the other hand, will look at the complete picture and will also look at the company's most recent accounts when assessing your ability to repay a loan.

Affect on Share Value

The value of a company is usually based on a multiple of its after-tax profits. A small minority shareholder's stake, however, is often valued according to the dividend history of the company. A consistent or steadily increasing annual dividend will enhance the value of the shares.

Chapter 29

Paying Salaries & Dividends: Profits & Paperwork

Salaries – Real Time Information

Since April 2013 employers have had to report salary payments to HMRC under the Real Time Information (RTI) regime. Under real time information, employers are required to submit a Full Payment Submission (FPS) to HMRC at the same time or before each payment is made to a director or employee.

The idea is to make sure the right amount of tax is paid at the right time. Under the previous system, employers generally only had to report payroll information to HMRC at the end of the year.

Under RTI the directors own salaries could result in additional payroll costs (for example, in small husband and wife companies or 'one man band' companies, where the only salaries paid are those of the directors themselves).

Where the directors receive small salaries, it may be cheaper and easier to register with HMRC as an annual scheme and pay salaries as a single annual lump sum (e.g. in March just before the end of the tax year).

With annual schemes an FPS is only expected in the month of payment and HMRC only has to be paid once a year. However, it is only possible to register as an annual scheme if all employees are paid annually at the same time.

Once a business is registered as an annual scheme, an Employer Payment Summary (EPS) is not required for the 11 months of the tax year where no payments are made to the directors. Schemes not registered as annual schemes have to make monthly submissions, even if no salaries are paid.

An additional problem may arise where directors withdraw cash from their companies and only later decide how these payments are to be treated (for example, as salaries or dividends).

Where the director's loan account is overdrawn, an amount withdrawn and subsequently designated as salary could result in a late filing penalty under RTI.

When directors withdraw money from their companies it is essential to decide up front the nature of the payment (e.g. salary, loan, dividend, reimbursement of expenses) and to have evidence supporting that decision.

For example, where a director borrows money from the company, the terms of the loan should be set out in writing. Withdrawals by directors that cannot be categorised might be treated as earnings by HMRC unless the company can prove otherwise.

Dividends

Distributable Profits

Under the Companies Act a company cannot legally pay a dividend unless it has sufficient distributable profits to cover it.

A company's distributable profits are its accumulated profits, less accumulated losses. This information can generally be found in the company's most recent annual accounts.

It is not necessary for the company to actually make a profit in the year the dividend is paid, as long as there are sufficient accumulated profits (after tax) from previous years.

If the distributable profits are not big enough to cover the dividend it may be necessary to prepare interim management accounts to justify the payment.

Before paying any dividends it is probably wise to speak to your accountant to check whether the company does indeed have sufficient distributable profits.

It may also be wise to check whether a loss has been realised since the last accounts were drawn up and whether any dividend will cause cash flow problems for the company.

In general, it is wise to be conservative and keep dividends to a reasonable level.

If the company does not have sufficient distributable profits to cover its dividend payments, the dividends will be illegal.

Illegal dividends have harmful tax and non-tax consequences. For example, the dividend may be treated as a loan which may be subject to the section 455 tax charge (see Chapter 22).

Dividend Formalities & Paperwork

It is possible that HMRC will try to tax dividends as employment income. To help avoid any such challenge it is essential to ensure that dividends are properly declared and you have the supporting paperwork to prove it.

This includes:

- Holding a directors' board meeting to recommend the dividend payment (with printed minutes to prove the meeting took place)

- Holding a general meeting of the company's members (i.e. shareholders) to approve the dividend payment (with printed minutes to prove the meeting took place).

- Issuing a dividend voucher to each shareholder.

Chapter 30

Dividends Taxed as Earnings

Recent tax cases demonstrate the potential danger that dividends paid to a director/shareholder may in some circumstances be vulnerable to a national insurance liability and possibly a full PAYE charge.

It remains to be seen how HMRC will choose to use these decisions in the context of family companies:

P A Holdings

PA Holdings switched from a conventional bonus arrangement to a more intricate structure whereby an employee benefit trust was funded by the company, which in turn awarded preference shares to employees. These preference shares duly paid a dividend after which they were redeemed.

The company and its employees argued that the dividends should be taxed as dividends using dividend tax rates and without any PAYE or national insurance implications.

By contrast, HMRC took the view that the dividends simply amounted to earnings and that the normal PAYE and national insurance payments should have been deducted from them and accounted for to HMRC.

The Court of Appeal overturned the decisions of the First Tier Tribunal and the Upper Tribunal and decided that the dividends were indeed earnings for employment and should therefore suffer deductions of income tax at source through PAYE. Both employers and employees national insurance deductions should also have been made.

PA Holdings initially decided to appeal to the Supreme Court but later threw in the towel. This led to fears that HMRC could attack director/shareholders who take most of their income as dividends.

Many tax advisers argue that the aggressive tax planning undertaken by PA Holdings (trying to change bonuses into dividends for a large chunk of employees) is entirely different to the profit extraction model of most small companies.

In other words, most director/shareholders should be able to continue paying themselves small salaries and taking the rest of their income as dividends with limited risk of challenge from HMRC.

Uniplex (UK) Ltd

Uniplex was sold a scheme aimed at giving employees dividend income instead of remuneration, issuing different classes of share to each employee. This type of arrangement is generally known as alphabet shares.

The scheme failed as it was not implemented as planned. However, the First Tier Tribunal judge added that the scheme, even if implemented correctly, might still have failed.

Stewart Fraser Ltd

This case involved a write off of loans by a close company to an employee shareholder. The loan write offs were treated as distributions taxable on the employee. HMRC successfully argued that national insurance liabilities were payable by the company on the loan write offs.

Practical Implications

The practical implications relate to the boundary between normal dividend payments and those which under the PA Holdings/Uniplex/Stewart Fraser case principles would be treated as employment earnings and hence attract income tax and national insurance deductions through PAYE. For instance in PA Holdings the First Tier Tribunal said:

"if something is paid out as a distribution by a company to an investing shareholder then the issue of derivation may arise if the shareholder is also an employee. The facts may show that the derivation of a dividend

from a share may not be related to earnings because the acquisition and ownership of the share was not related to earnings or more generally to the status of the individual as an employee of the company".

In Uniplex, the First Tier Tribunal said:

"The PA Holdings case is authority for the proposition that payments from a party other than the employer can be from an employee's employment" and *"It may well have still been the case that the full amount would have been taxable because employees had given no consideration for the payment other than their services".*

Summary

Dividends paid to an employee-shareholder may in some circumstances be vulnerable to a national insurance liability, and possibly to a full PAYE charge. It remains to be seen how HMRC will choose to use these decisions in the contexts of family companies and remuneration planning generally.

Chapter 31

Small Salary, Big Dividends: Potential Dangers

It is quite common practice for company owners to pay themselves a small salary and take the rest of their income as dividends. Many accountants have been recommending this strategy for years.

However, it is important to point out that some tax advisors are cautious about certain aspects of this tax planning technique, especially in light of recent court decisions like *PA Holdings*, where the Court of Appeal decided that certain dividends should be subject to PAYE and national insurance (see Chapter 30).

There is a fear that cases like this will create a wide precedent for any employer that pays dividends to its staff. It is difficult to quantify the potential danger, however, because a lot depends on HMRC's willingness to act. The most vulnerable, arguably, are those that use tax planning techniques that HMRC may view as aggressive, including possibly:

- Large scale contrived arrangements where dividends are created for tax avoidance purposes (as in *PA Holdings*).

- Directors' loans that are written off and taxed as dividends.

- Dividend waivers that are used to divert income to other shareholders, for example where a director waives his own dividends so that his wife can receive more tax-free income. HMRC recently succeeded in challenging dividend waivers in the case of *Donovan & McLaren v HMRC*.

- Certain 'Alphabet' share arrangements, where different classes of shares (A, B, C etc) have no substantive rights other than to dividends. These arrangements are often used to substitute dividends for bonuses.

- Situations where previous salaries have been reduced in favour of dividends.

The sixty-four thousand dollar question is: where does this leave the average small company owner taking a small salary and the rest of his income as dividends?

At the time of writing it would appear that most small companies are not under attack but this state of affairs could change at any time. The small salary/big dividend tax planning technique does not produce *guaranteed* tax savings. There is a danger, no matter how small, that HMRC may try to tax your dividends as earnings, if not now then at some point in the future.

Also, with regards to the last point in the above list, please note that some (more conservative) tax advisors argue that if you are currently taking a salary that is larger than the 'optimal' amounts listed in Chapter 6 you should not reduce it.

There is also a danger that at some point in the future legislation could be introduced that imposes heavier tax on dividends from close companies. This could completely negate many of the tax benefits of running your business as a limited company.

Chapter 32

Personal Service Companies

If your company is classed as a personal service company, many of the tax planning opportunities available to other company owners may not be available, for example, the ability to take dividends that are free from national insurance.

Personal service companies have to operate the infamous 'IR35' regime which means the company may be forced to calculate a notional salary for the director/shareholder.

This deemed income will be subject to PAYE and national insurance.

Essentially, HMRC may ignore the company set up and treat most of the company's income as employment income.

Which Companies Are Affected by IR35?

This is where it all becomes a bit of a grey area (which is why professional advice is essential!)

A personal service company is, generally speaking, a firm that receives all or most of its income from services provided by the director/shareholder.

Often the work will be carried out for just one client, often for a long period of time, and the client will probably only want the personal services of the company owner (hence IR35 often applies to 'one man band' companies).

Essentially HMRC is looking for cases of 'disguised employment'. In other words, ignoring the fact that there is an intermediary company, the relationship is more like an employer/employee relationship rather than the kind of relationship that exists between independent self-employed business owners and their clients.

Where such 'disguised employment' exists, the company must apply the IR35 regime to the payments received from that client – effectively treating most of those payments as if they were salary paid to the director/shareholder.

A typical situation which might be caught under the IR35 rules is where the individual resigns as an employee and then goes back to the same job but working through a company.

However, it's all very subjective with a long line of legal cases adding to the confusion.

Personal service companies can be found in many different business sectors: the most cited example is IT consultants.

They also came under the media spotlight in recent times when it was disclosed that some BBC presenters had been operating as 'freelancers' via personal service companies, when many would argue that they are in fact nothing but employees of the BBC.

Business Entity Tests

In May 2012 HMRC published a set of 'business entity tests' that are being piloted to help companies assess whether they should be applying the IR35 rules.

Essentially the tests attempt to distinguish between companies that are truly independent businesses and those that are simply employment in another guise.

There are 12 tests with different points attached to each. By adding up the total points, you can assess which risk band you fall into:

Less than 10 points	High risk
10 to 20 points	Medium risk
More than 20 points	Low risk

If HMRC checks whether IR35 applies to you, and you can prove that you are in the low risk band, they will generally close their IR35 review.

The tests are as follows:

1. Business Premises Test. Does your business own or rent business premises which are separate both from your home and from the end client's premises? *Score 10 points if the answer is yes.*

2. PII Test. Do you need professional indemnity insurance? *Score 2 points if the answer is yes.*

3. Efficiency Test. Has your business had the opportunity in the last 24 months to increase its income by working more efficiently (e.g. contract clauses that pay you a fixed amount for a job even if you finish early)? *Score 10 points if the answer is yes.*

4. Assistance Test. Does your business engage any workers (other than the directors/shareholders) who bring in at least 25% of the yearly turnover? *Score 35 points if the answer is yes.*

5. Advertising Test. Has your business spent over £1,200 on advertising in the last 12 months? *Score 2 points if the answer is yes.*

6. Previous PAYE Test. Has the current client engaged you on PAYE employment terms within the 12 months which ended on the last 31 March, with no major changes to your working arrangements? *Score minus 15 points if answer is yes.*

7. Business Plan Test. Does your business have a business plan with a cash flow forecast which you update regularly? Does your business have a business bank account, identified as such by the bank, which is separate from your personal account? *Score 1 point if your answer to both questions is yes.*

8. Repair at Own Expense. Would your business have to bear the cost of having to put right any mistakes? *Score 4 points if your answer is yes.*

9. Client Risk Test. Has your business been unable to recover payment:
  * For work done in the last 24 months
  * More than 10% of yearly turnover?

Score 10 points if your answer is yes.

10. Billing Test. Do you invoice for work carried out before being paid and negotiate payment terms? *Score 2 points if your answer is yes.*

11. Right of Substitution Test. Does your business have the right to send a substitute? *Score 2 points if your answer is yes.*

12. Actual Substitution Test. Have you hired anyone in the last 24 months to do the work you have taken on? *Score 20 points if the answer is yes.*

These tests may provide a useful guide and indicate whether HMRC might want to investigate your tax affairs.

However, they are purely guidance and not based on law. The actual application of IR35 will always boil down to individual engagements and each contract must be looked at separately.

Ultimately, professional advice will still be required to determine whether you are subject to IR35 or not.

Part 9

More Tax Planning Ideas

Chapter 33

How to Pay 18% CGT by Postponing Dividends

Under the current capital gains tax rules there are three tax rates:

- 10% where Entrepreneurs Relief applies
- 18% for other gains made by basic-rate taxpayers
- 28% for other gains made by higher-rate taxpayers

We looked at Entrepreneurs Relief in Chapter 25.

In all other cases, the amount of capital gains tax you pay depends on how much income you have earned during the tax year.

The maximum amount of capital gains that you can have taxed at 18% during the current tax year is £31,865. This is the amount of the basic-rate tax band for 2014/15.

Basic-rate taxpayers pay 10% less capital gains tax than higher-rate taxpayers. This means the basic-rate tax band can save each person up to £3,187 in capital gains tax this year:

$$£31,865 \times 10\% = £3,187$$

This creates some interesting tax-planning opportunities:

Income Planning

If you expect to realise a large capital gain, for example by disposing of a buy-to-let property, you may be able to save quite a lot of tax by making sure the disposal takes place during a tax year in which your taxable income is quite low.

In this respect, company owners can manipulate their incomes more easily than regular employees, sole traders or business partners.

The company itself can keep trading and generating profits but the company owner can make sure that very little of these profits are extracted and taxed in his or her hands.

Example

Richard, a company owner, sells a buy-to-let property, realising a gain of £50,000 after deducting all buying and selling costs. Deducting his annual CGT exemption of £11,000 leaves a taxable gain of £39,000.

Richard hasn't paid himself any dividends during the current tax year and decides to postpone paying any so that £31,865 of his capital gain is taxed at 18%. The remaining £7,135 will be taxed at 28%. This simple piece of tax planning saves Richard £3,187 in capital gains tax.

Note that Richard can still pay himself a tax-free salary of up to £10,000 to utilise his income tax personal allowance. The income tax personal allowance does not interfere with the capital gains tax calculation. (In practice he may be better off paying himself a slightly smaller salary of £7,956 if his company doesn't have any spare employment allowance.)

Limitations

Although postponing dividends could help you pay less capital gains tax, it's probably not worth doing this unless you can withdraw the postponed dividends tax free in a future tax year. If you take a bigger dividend in a later tax year, and end up paying 25% income tax, you may end up worse off overall.

Example continued

In the above example Richard postponed taking a gross dividend of £31,865 to free up his basic-rate band and pay 18% capital gains tax.

If during 2015/16 he takes an additional dividend of £31,865, on top off his usual salary and tax-free dividends, he will pay income tax of £7,170 (£31,865 x 22.5%). He saved £3,187 in capital gains tax in 2014/15 but pays an additional £7,170 of income tax in 2015/16. Overall Richard is £3,983 worse off.

Chapter 34

Emigrating to Avoid Tax

Possibly the most drastic step you can take to avoid tax is leave the country!

By becoming non-resident you may be able to avoid both capital gains tax (when you sell your company) and income tax (if you want to withdraw big dividends).

Capital Gains Tax

In the past it was possible to go and live in certain countries for just one year and completely avoid paying capital gains tax.

This was a fantastic loophole, especially when capital gains tax was levied at rates of up to 40%.

Unfortunately that loophole was closed and most UK taxpayers who move abroad temporarily to avoid capital gains tax will be taxed when they return, if the period of non residence lasts for five years or less. (This is a change from the previous anti-avoidance rule which applied if there were fewer than five complete tax years between the year of departure and the year of return.)

With a capital gains tax rate of just 10% applying to many company sales (where Entrepreneurs Relief applies), many company owners would be unwilling to exile themselves from the UK for five years just to increase their bank accounts by 10%.

Moving abroad is an expensive and time-consuming business and these costs would eat into your tax savings.

Of course, if you plan to emigrate one day anyway, this is all academic. You may be able to live in the country of your dreams **and** avoid paying tax at the same time.

Income Tax

Where a company has built up significant distributable profits it has been possible in the past to withdraw these profits as tax-free dividends during a short period of non-residence.

This tax planning opportunity is no longer available following the introduction of some new anti-avoidance rules. Income from "closely controlled companies" (most small companies) will be taxed if the recipient becomes UK resident again after a temporary period of non residence of five years or less.

This anti-avoidance rule does not apply to dividends paid out of "post-departure" profits, ie profits built up while you are non-resident.

It is not meant to apply to employment and self-employment earnings or regular investment income, eg dividends from stock market companies and bank interest.

Furthermore, the anti-avoidance rule will only apply where an individual has been resident in four or more of the seven tax years prior to the tax year in which they become non-resident.

While it may no longer be possible to avoid income tax by becoming non-resident for a short period, this tax planning strategy may still work for genuine emigrants who decide to leave the UK permanently.

However, at the time of writing the precise workings of this new anti-avoidance provision were unclear. Professional advice should be obtained before attempting to become non-resident to reduce UK taxes.

Statutory Residence Test

So how do you become non-resident?

A new statutory residence test has been in operation since 6 April 2013. This test is supposed to make it a lot easier to determine your residence status and hence where you stand when it comes to paying UK tax. Whether it will achieve this aim remains to be seen.

Automatic Overseas Tests

You start with the automatic overseas tests. You will be automatically *non-resident* for the tax year if you meet *any* of the following tests:

- You spend fewer than 16 days in the UK during the tax year. This test is used if you were UK resident in *any* of the previous 3 tax years.

- You spend fewer than 46 days in the UK during the tax year. This test is used if you were UK resident in *none* of the previous three tax years.

- If you work sufficient hours overseas (generally 35 hours or more per week on average) without a significant break, and during the tax year:

  - ➤ You spend fewer than 91 days in the UK, and
  - ➤ You spend fewer than 31 days working in the UK (a work day means more than three hours work).

If you do not meet any of these automatic overseas tests, you should move onto the 'automatic UK tests'.

Automatic UK Tests

You will be automatically *UK resident* for the tax year if you meet *any* of the following tests:

- You spend 183 days or more in the UK during the tax year.

- You have a home in the UK and are present in that home on 30 or more days during the tax year. This test only applies if you do not have an overseas home or, if you do have an overseas home, you are present in that home on fewer than 30 days during the tax year.

- You work full time in the UK for any period of 365 days (all or part of which falls into the tax year) with no significant break.

If any of the automatic UK tests apply to you for a particular tax year and none of the automatic overseas tests apply, you are UK resident for tax purposes for that tax year.

If you do not meet any of the automatic overseas tests and do not meet any of the automatic UK tests you have to use the sufficient ties test to determine your residence status for the tax year.

Sufficient Ties Test

This test takes into account your UK ties and the number of days you spend in the UK. The more ties you have, the more likely it is that you will be UK resident for tax purposes:

- **Family tie** – your spouse or common-law partner (unless separated) or children under 18 (with some exceptions) are UK resident.

- **Accommodation tie** – you have a place to live in the UK that is available for a continuous period of 91 days or more during the tax year. You don't have to own the property but must spend at least one night there during the tax year or, if it is the home of a close relative, you must spend at least 16 nights in it to have an accommodation tie.

- **Work tie** – you do more than three hours work a day in the UK for a total of at least 40 days. Includes employment and self-employment.

- **90-day tie** – you have spent more than 90 days in the UK in either or both of the previous two tax years.

- **Country tie** – the UK is the country in which you were present for the greatest number of days during the tax year. This tie only applies if you were UK resident in any of the previous three tax years.

These ties are then combined with days spent in the UK to determine your residence status.

The scoring is different for people who have recently left the UK (i.e. were UK resident in any of the previous three tax years) and those who have recently arrived (i.e. were not resident in any of the previous three tax years).

UK Resident in Any of Previous 3 Tax Years – Leavers

UK ties are combined with days spent in the UK as follows:

Days in UK	Residence status
Fewer than 16 days	Always non-resident
16 – 45 days	UK Resident if 4 or more ties
46 – 90 days	UK Resident if 3 or more ties
91 – 120 days	UK Resident if 2 or more ties
121-182 days	UK Resident if 1 or more ties
183 days or more	Always UK resident

Not Resident in All 3 Previous Tax Years – Arrivers

UK ties are combined with days spent in the UK as follows:

Days in UK	Resident Status
Fewer than 16 days	Always non-resident
16 – 45 days	Always non-resident
46 – 90 days	UK resident if all 4 ties
91 – 120 days	UK resident if 3 or more ties
121-182 days	UK resident if 2 or more ties
183 days or more	Always UK resident

Further Information

Finally, please note that many of the terms used in this chapter have complex definitions and there is more to the statutory residence test than can be covered in just a few pages.

For more information see the Taxcafe guide *Non-Resident & Offshore Tax Planning*.